GERALD D. IVERSON

ways to plan & organize your Sunday School

adult

INTERNATIONAL CENTER FOR LEARNING

A Division of G/L Publications, Glendale, California, U.S.A.

BV
1488
.193
1973

ᶜ Copyright 1971 by G/L Publications. All rights reserved. Printed in U.S.A.

Published by Regal Books Division, G/L Publications, Glendale, California 91209, U.S.A.
Library of Congress Catalog Card No. 70-168841. ISBN 0-8307-0125-7

Photo credits: Page 34: David J. Pavol.
All other photos: Douglas Gilbert.

CONTENTS

Training materials for use with this handbook
are available from your church supplier.

THE AUTHOR

Gerald D. Iverson graduated in sociology from Westmont College and received the MRE from Fuller Theological Seminary.

Gerry is an experienced director of Christian education, having held this position in Baptist churches on the West Coast. He is presently serving on the Christian education board of his church and teaching an adult class. Gerry and Janie Iverson have two children.

Since completing the material for this book, Mr. Iverson has joined the G/L Publications staff as an editor for the award-winning TEACH magazine.

FOREWORD

The late Dr. Henrietta C. Mears, founder of Gospel Light Publications and distinguished Christian education leader for more than 40 years, often said, "Good teachers are not born; they are made by conscientious labor." It is axiomatic that if one is to be successful in any field, he must be trained. Our Lord recognized this fact in training the Twelve. First He spent the whole night in prayer in preparation for the momentous task of choosing them. From this point the teaching and training of these men became a matter of paramount importance to Him.

A tremendous passion for the training of leadership has been a hallmark in the program of Gospel Light. What workers learn today will determine what the church will be tomorrow. This is the great need of the hour; to train leaders for Christian service, and particularly the Sunday school, people who will know how to administer and teach. With a deep sense of obligation as well as opportunity the International Center for Learning was created in 1970 to specialize in the training of dedicated personnel in all departments of the local church.

This is one of a series of textbooks designed to train workers in the Sunday school. It has grown out of actual proven experience and represents the best educational philosophy. In addition to textual materials, the full program of ICL includes audio visual media and church leadership training seminars sponsored in strategic centers across America and ultimately overseas as rapidly as God enables. We are being deluged with requests to help in the momentous task of training workers. We dare not stop short of providing all possible assistance.

Train for Sunday school success! Train for church growth! Train people by example and experience to pray and plan and perform. Christ trained the Twelve. Dare we do less?

President, Gospel Light Publications

It was hot. Really hot. The young stranger and his friends had been traveling on foot for several hours. And now he sat by a well while his friends went to a neighboring village for supplies.

A solitary figure bearing a waterpot approached the well. Her sandled feet scuffed little puffs of dust about her ankles as she nervously quickened her pace. Both were aware of one another's presence.

The young stranger broke the silence. He said to her, "Give Me a drink."[1]

A dialogue followed which was to radically change the life-style of this common woman of the streets.

As the stranger's friends were returning, the woman rushed past them and into the village; she had been so anxious to return that she had left her waterpot behind.

As the stranger from Nazareth conversed with his friends by the well, the voices of the excited townspeople were lofted to them on the warm Palestinian breeze.

Jesus tossed his head in the direction of the approaching crowd and said to his disciples, ". . . Lift up your eyes, and look on the fields, that they are white for harvest."[2]

Jesus wasn't talking about farming. He was talking about people. "Look around you! Vast fields of human souls are ripening all around us, and are ready now for reaping."[3]

The villagers welcomed the Teacher because of the woman's testimony; Jesus remained in the village for two days while the people gladly heard him. "And many more believed because of His word."[4]

Little has changed. In the words of Sisemore, "Adults face perennial pressures, treacherous temptations, perplexing problems and relentless responsibilities."[5]

Many adults feel that they do not have adequate resources to cope with modern-day living. And they don't! There is great frustration and restlessness in the hearts of men today. They are longing for a word from God. They are longing for the love and acceptance which the people in our churches can give them. They are crying out within their hearts to be released from the despair of loneliness which grips them.

Adults *can* be reached for Jesus Christ. Adults *must* be reached for Jesus Christ. And many adults *want* to be reached for Christ.

There are more than ninety million adults in the United States who are not enrolled in Sunday school—adults who are groping in the darkness for a touch of the Master's hand.

Sisemore writes with insight when he says: "Churches have justified their neglect of adults by proclaiming that the children are the church of tomorrow. To be sure, this concept is true; but it is only a part of a larger truth. The full truth is this: The children are the hope of *the day after tomorrow*, the youth are the hope of *tomorrow*, but adults are the only hope for *today*. Lose the children and the church will die in *two* generations; lose the youth, and the church will die in *one* generation; lose the adults, and the church may very well die in *this* generation! Who could deny that the current moral, social and theological conflicts are largely, if not totally, the result of the failure to meaningfully reach adults for Christ and adequately involve them in Christian education?"[3]

Adults provide the leadership for the entire church. It is adults who, through their faithful stewardship, provide the financial backing for the church and missions program. Adults are responsible for the spiritual nurture of their children, whether it be as teachers and leaders through the ministry of our Sunday school or through the ministry of the home as loving, concerned parents.

It is time to take positive action in developing the adult area of our Sunday schools. That's what this book is all about: to help you plan and organize your Sunday school so that it is meaningful, exciting, and meeting the needs of your adults.

Our Sunday schools must produce disciples of Jesus Christ.

The primary definition of the word *disciple* is "a learner." Learning must take place in our Sunday schools if we are to produce disciples of Jesus Christ. Adults need to learn; they need to become disciples of Jesus Christ.

They need to learn the Bible. They need to learn to "walk in the Spirit" (Galatians 5:16). Adults need to learn how to share their faith in Jesus Christ with others. They need to learn how to establish a Christian home and to learn what it means to be Christian parents. Adults need to learn to develop spiritual values in our secular, materialistic culture. They need to learn how to handle the problems and frustrations of day-to-day living. They need to learn to make Jesus Christ the Lord of all areas of their lives.

In short, adults need to learn to experience the abundant life offered by Jesus Christ. Adult Sunday school should be the medium which bridges the gap between theology and life as we live it.

In planning and organizing the adult Sunday school, we must recognize the value in breaking away from stereotyped teaching methods. There are teaching methods equally as valid as the traditional lecture method; methods which will provide you as a teacher with "feedback," allowing you to assess how well you are communicating the Word of God. We must organize and plan for the free, creative use of the Sunday school session. We refer you to the companion volume in this series, *Ways to Help Them Learn: Adult,* by H. Norman Wright, for the discussion of teaching methods.

Developing disciples of Jesus Christ does not take place by accident but by design. And it is not done simply. We must marshal all of the talents and abilities that God has given us to plan and organize our adult Sunday school so that the Spirit of God can freely use it to accomplish His purposes.

To this end we wish you Godspeed.

FOOTNOTES

PREFACE

1 • John 4:7, *New American Standard Bible.* ℂ The Lockman Foundation, 1971. Used by permission.

2 • John 4:35, *NASB.*

3 • John 4:35, *The Living Bible,* Paraphrased (Wheaton: Tyndale House, publishers, 1971). Used by permission.

4 • John 4:41, *NASB.*

5 • Roy B. Zuck and Gene A. Getz, *Adult Education in the Church* (Chicago: Moody Press, 1970), p. 13.

6 • Zuck and Betz, *Adult Education in the Church,* pp. 14-15.

WHAT ARE WE DOING HERE?

Jim and Sandy Taylor sat in their adult Sunday school classroom with their Bibles on their laps. Across from them sat Paul and Vicki Hamilton. Jim, the teacher, shrugged his shoulders in disappointment.

"Another Sunday morning down the tubes," he complained. "Four of us meeting out of a potential of hundreds."

"What's wrong with this class?" Sandy asked. "Why don't people come and get involved?"

There was a moment of silence as the four thought about this question.

"Listen," Jim said, finally. "I've got an idea!"

"Shoot!" Paul encouraged him. "We're willing to help in any way we can."

Jim got up and walked over to the chalkboard on the wall. "First of all, we have no objectives in this class. What I mean is, what are we doing here? What is this Sunday school class trying to accomplish? Let's make a list on the board. Paul, what exactly do you think a Sunday school is all about? Vicki and Sandy, you do the same thinking. Let's be clear about what we're trying to do before we try to do it!"

Basically, the adult division of Sunday school has four main objectives it is trying to accomplish. These are:

1 To reach prospective class members.

2 To produce an atmosphere of warmth and acceptance.

3 To provide sound biblical instruction.

4 To promote daily application of biblical material.

Each objective, of course, is partially determined by the other three. You cannot have sound biblical instruction unless you have class members to instruct. And you cannot reach prospective members unless the atmosphere within your class makes them want to become active participants. Each objective, then, partially depends on the others for fulfillment.

"We're on the right track!" Jim exclaimed. "Now let's find out a little more about each of these objectives."

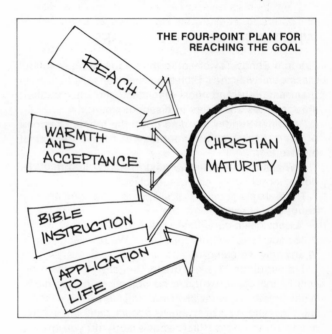

THE FOUR-POINT PLAN FOR REACHING THE GOAL

REACH

WARMTH AND ACCEPTANCE

BIBLE INSTRUCTION

APPLICATION TO LIFE

CHRISTIAN MATURITY

TO REACH PROSPECTIVE CLASS MEMBERS

It may seem elementary to say that one must have pupils in order to have a school, but many churches have no planned program for reaching and for recruiting prospective class members at all! They seem to assume that it is the teacher's responsibility to attract new members, while some teachers obviously operate upon the assumption that the pupils in his class will bring their friends and acquaintances. And others take it for granted that the real key to Sunday school growth lies with the pastor. So we all tend to look at one another, pass the buck, and stagnate.

"That's one of the real problems with this class," Paul admitted. "I admit that I haven't invited anyone to Sunday school in a long time. But I guess the problem is that I don't know how to do it. I always get tongue-tied when I try to invite someone to church or Sunday school."

"My problem is different," said Sandy. "I just don't know where to meet people who would be good prospects for this class."

"I guess I'm just lazy," Vicki admitted. "I know plenty of people who should be in this class, but I just don't take the time or energy to go and invite them."

Jim made a list on the chalkboard that read like this:

Problems in Reaching New Class Members

1 Inability to witness on a one-to-one basis.

2 Lack of confrontation with people who would be potential members.

3 Lack of discipline in spending time inviting people to Sunday school.

"There are ways to reach prospective class members," Jim offered. "Success in a Sunday school doesn't happen by accident. Let's think about some of these ways to reach people."

Prospective class members are reached basically in one of two ways: by an individual or by the class as a whole. Many people feel panicky, like Paul Hamilton, when someone starts talking about individual responsibility in reaching prospective class members. They conjure up the image of "buttonholing" someone and asking him, "Are you saved, brother?" assuming that the only way of reaching class members is to persuade unbelievers to come to Sunday school and church to "get religion."

But the Sunday school must reach the "reached" as well as the "unreached." In most churches there is a large segment of the adult membership that never attends Sunday school. These people are in desperate need of Sunday school. (They may be totally unaware of that need, however.) Reaching the prospective class member includes "inreach" as well as "outreach."

Believers who have recently moved into a new neighborhood are also candidates for membership in Sunday school. People are sometimes rather slow in finding a new church home when they have moved; how satisfying it can be when their new church home finds them through the ministry of a concerned adult Sunday school class member!

This is not to minimize the importance of personal evangelism or sharing our faith with those who don't know Jesus Christ as Lord and Saviour. But it should be remembered that believers and church members who don't attend Sunday school are to be considered prospective class members too.

"Let's make a list of the possibilities," Jim encouraged. He wrote the following on the board:

The "Reached" We Need to Reach:

1 Church members who do not attend Sunday school on a regular basis.

2 Believers in the neighborhood who do not attend a church regularly.

3 New neighbors in the community who are believers.

REACHING THE "UNREACHED"

Another way to reach prospective class members is for individuals to share their faith with unbelievers, lead them to a saving knowledge of the Lord Jesus Christ, and bring them to Sunday school and church as a natural follow-up. These new babes in Christ will need the spiritual nurture provided by our Sunday school classes and the fellowship with other believers.

The fact that personal evangelism is a frightening experience for some Christians may indicate that our churches have not been equipping us for performing this ministry of ". . . the word of reconciliation."[1] Often people are too uncomfortable with the other members of their class to share these difficulties and fears of witnessing and living a Christian life; there is a fear of appearing "unspiritual" in the eyes of our fellow class members.

But the fact remains that personal evangelism is a vital means of reaching prospective class members, and our Sunday school classes should be equipping members to do this very thing!

"Well, we've decided we need to reach the 'reached' and the 'unreached,' " Jim said. "But our class has no organized method to do so."

"Visitation!" one of the young women remarked. "Let's talk about a visitation program!"

An effective visitation program is vital to the Sunday school. Several class members or one or two couples can help reach prospective class members by taking one or two evenings in the week to seek out and fellowship with these people. When the joy, warmth, and compassion of Christ are expressed in initial encounters with prospective class members, they will be highly motivated to accept the invitation to attend a Sunday school class and church. The prospects will be much more inclined to attend because they won't feel like total strangers the first time they come; there will be several familiar faces among the new group of people.

Visitation after the first time guests attend the Sunday school is helpful also. It insures a second return and shows the guests that they are sincerely wanted. Too often a class's visitation program melts after the first encounter, leaving the prospective members up in the air. Follow-through on visitation is just as important as the initial visit.

"Okay," Jim said, "we've got a good start. I'm going to write on the board all the things we can do to reach prospective class members."

Reaching Prospective Class Members:

1 Contact people in the church who do not attend a Sunday school class.

2 Contact new residents in the community who may not know of your particular church.

3 Contact believers in the community who do not have a church home as yet.

4 Set up a regular, systematic visitation program.

5 Encourage and teach individual witnessing to bring

FIVE SOURCES OF NEW CLASS MEMBERS

- ☑ NON-ATTENDING CHURCH MEMBERS
- ☑ NEW RESIDENTS IN THE COMMUNITY
- ☑ UNCHURCHED BELIEVERS
- ☑ VISITATION PROGRAM CONTACTS
- ☑ INDIVIDUAL WITNESSING CONTACTS

others to Christ—and then to church and Sunday school.

"Objective Number One," Jim stated, "has been agreed upon. We need to be reaching prospective class members. Now for Objective Number Two: What do we do to make sure that these new members continue to come to our Sunday school class?

"Good question!" Paul agreed. "We've had so many people come to class one time and then disappear off the face of the earth. What are we doing wrong?"

"Maybe it has something to do with the atmosphere in the class," Sandy ventured. "Maybe we ought to make them feel more comfortable than we do."

"I agree," Jim said. "And I think that should be the second objective for our Sunday school."

TO PRODUCE AN ATMOSPHERE OF WARMTH AND ACCEPTANCE

Each individual has basic personal needs which can be met by other human beings. It has been observed that three of these needs are: (1) the need for attention, (2) the need for acceptance, and (3) the need for affection.

RECOGNIZING MODERN ISOLATION

A great deal in contemporary society prevents the satisfaction of these needs. Computer-age technology tends to obscure one's individual identity behind a pattern of numbers on an IBM card. Approximately 27 percent of the population of the U.S. moves its residence every year, leaving friends and associates behind again and again. Sociologists state that this mobility results in people being set adrift on a sea of anonymity. Loneliness and a feeling of isolation have become characteristics of modern existence, and people don't like it.

LOVING AWAY ISOLATION

The Lord Jesus told His disciples that love is the sure sign of discipleship.[2] And the love of which He was speaking is "a love springing from a sense of the preciousness of the object loved." Loving people means paying attention to them, not being indifferent toward them. Loving people means accepting them in spite of their problems and personality quirks. Loving people means being affectionate with them. The people in the

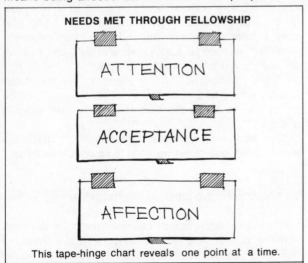

NEEDS MET THROUGH FELLOWSHIP

ATTENTION

ACCEPTANCE

AFFECTION

This tape-hinge chart reveals one point at a time.

Church of Jesus Christ should do much to meet in a Christian manner the basic needs of the individuals in their fellowship.

"This raises some interesting questions," Jim remarked. "Let's write them down."

1 Are we producing an atmosphere of warmth and acceptance?

2 How do people feel as they enter our Sunday school classroom?

3 Do they feel a part of the group?

4 Do they feel welcome?

5 Do they receive positive attention from the group?

6 Do they leave with a feeling of personal worth and a sense that they have been recognized and appreciated as individuals?

7 Or do they feel like intruders or outsiders?

8 Are they confronted with "fellowship groups" so closely knit as to be some sort of "spiritual cliques" into which it is practically impossible to break?

There should be an understanding among the class members that any visitors will be warmly accepted by all. The conditions which produce the needed atmosphere of warmth and acceptance can be planned and arranged for. They usually do not happen by accident. Prayerful consideration should be given as to what can be done to give each individual a sense of being precious in both the sight of God and other class members.

"Wow!" exclaimed Sandy. "Now there's an objective we really need to be working toward!"

"Right," answered Jim. "It seems to me that if our Sunday school can meet these two objectives, it will be on its way to being the tool of God that He wants it to be."

"But let's not stop here," Paul urged. "There are several other objectives we need to be concerned with."

TO PROVIDE SOUND BIBLICAL INSTRUCTION

"Well, this objective mainly concerns me," Jim decided. "I'm the teacher. And I guess I've got a lot to learn about how God can use me in that role. But you know something? I'm more excited about teaching my class now than I have been in a long time."

"Okay, let's go on, then," Vicki said. "We've decided that Sunday school needs to reach prospective class members and make them feel warm. But how does the Sunday school teach them the truths of the Bible?"

DEPENDING UPON THE HOLY SPIRIT

It is the teacher's job to bring forth the particular Bible truths that a class is studying on any given Sunday. But it must be remembered that it is the Holy Spirit who makes that truth real in a class member's life. Once the teacher recognizes this fact, he will be freed from the pressure of having to "pound the truth" into his pupils' heads. He will learn to rely, through prayer and preparation, upon the power and thoroughness of the Holy Spirit.

As the teacher opens himself to the Spirit's teaching ability, he will discover previously unknown powers and talents. He will see results in the lives of his pupils that will assure him of God's presence in the classroom.

The Holy Spirit, then, teaches both the teacher and *AMEN!!* the students. Only He can provide the sound biblical instruction that is necessary in Sunday school.

MINIMIZING LECTURE METHOD

It needs to be recognized that sound biblical instruction means more than a mini-preaching service. The old teaching adage of "you sit still while I instill" doesn't work when it comes to providing the best conditions for adult learning.

The teacher who lectures to his class for the entire session runs the risk of losing his students' attention. Adults need to be challenged and confronted in the classroom into thinking through problems and offering solutions to them.

The exclusive use of the lecture method of teaching prevents a difference of opinion and viewpoint. Although someone in the class may have a valid interpretation or opinion, it is often left unsaid because there just isn't enough time to fit it in before, during, or after the teacher's lecture.

Thirdly, recollection of material given during a lecture period is much lower than it is with group participation. Statistics show that retention is significantly related to the amount of discussion and involvement the pupil has in the lesson.

Sound biblical instruction, then, is best achieved when the teacher seeks to actively involve his class members in the learning process.

RELYING UPON GROUP PARTICIPATION

Since the Holy Spirit indwells each Christian in a Sunday school class, the class member is capable of making as valid a contribution to the learning experience as the teacher is. It is necessary to make room in the classroom procedure for meaningful learning experiences such as discussion, buzz groups, circle response, neighbor nudging, and other forms of personal interaction among the various class members. *Ways to Help Them Learn: Adults* by H. Norman Wright, the companion book to this one, contains an in-depth discussion of teaching methodology effective with adults.

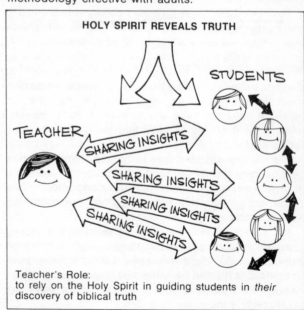

HOLY SPIRIT REVEALS TRUTH

STUDENTS

TEACHER

SHARING INSIGHTS
SHARING INSIGHTS
SHARING INSIGHTS
SHARING INSIGHTS

Teacher's Role:
to rely on the Holy Spirit in guiding students in *their* discovery of biblical truth

Jim was amazed. "This sheds a whole new light on teaching. I always thought a good teacher prepared a lesson during the week and then told it to the class on Sunday morning. I guess I never realized how much better it would be if everyone participated."

"And maybe that's why I feel like I don't really know what some of the other class members think," offered Sandy. "They never really do any of the talking."

"But there's one more objective," Paul stated. "I always forget the lesson when I walk out of Sunday school. Shouldn't we be applying the lessons in our day-to-day lives?"

"I think you're right, Paul," Jim agreed. "Let's make that our final objective for adult Sunday school."

TO PROMOTE DAILY APPLICATION OF BIBLICAL MATERIAL

What happens after the dismissal bell rings on Sunday morning? Sunday school is officially over and too often that ends it all. Class members venture forth from their classrooms with nothing but a nice warm feeling which they hope will sustain them until next week—same time, same station. But, as the lady sings it, "Is that all there is?" Or does God intend the precious truth of His Word to remain locked up within the hearts and minds of His people?

ENCOURAGING FAITH TO WORK

The answer to this, of course, is that Monday through Saturday should be affected by what has taken place on Sunday morning.

But many times people have stumbled into the pitfall of which James warns them. It is deceptive to think that what takes place in the classroom is all that really matters. James exhorts Christians to be "doers of the word and not hearers only."[4] Spiritual maturity and the love of Christ need to be expressed in concrete ways. James says that faith must be expressed in good works. "Even so faith, if it hath not works, is dead, being alone" and ". . . faith without works is dead."[5]

Each individual class member must be able to actively express his faith in the Lord Jesus Christ. Personal evangelism, visiting the sick and bereaved, assisting the elderly, and other service projects should be the natural outgrowth of and response to the sound biblical instruction in our classes. The Sunday school must provide the framework in which the truth of God's Word can be concretely expressed.

ENCOURAGING FAITH TO GROW

The outcome of promoting application of God's Word in class members' individual lives is that faith is increased. And as faith in Jesus Christ is increased, more and more people will be brought into God's kingdom by the witness of Sunday school adult members. As faith grows, the atmosphere of warmth and acceptance will become a natural part of Sunday school classroom environments. The circle of Sunday school objectives will be complete. Those who are brought to class as prospects will have the opportunity to become total disciples of Jesus Christ. They will have an opportunity to love and care for others and to melt the feelings of isolation which are so prevalent. But these opportunities will come only when biblical instruction is sound and made applicable to the pupils' daily lives.

READY . . . SET . . . GO!

"Well, that does it!" Jim exclaimed. "Those are the four objectives of the adult Sunday school."

"It's quite a handful," Paul commented.

"But it's exciting to know where we're going," Sandy added.

"And why," Vicki said.

"We're on the right track," Jim cautioned, "but we're not through by any means. We still have a lot to learn about adult Sunday school."

"Say, I have an idea!" Vicki said. "Why don't you and Sandy come over Tuesday night and we'll tackle the next step in organizing this class."

"Fine," Jim answered. "But first let's decide what the

next step is so that we can all be thinking about it before Tuesday.''

''And we ought to have Tom Sanders over too, since he's Sunday school superintendent,'' Sandy mentioned.

They all agreed that Tom should be in on their Tuesday night meeting.

''Remember the four objectives for adult Sunday school,'' Jim stated.

---

1 **To Reach Prospective Class Members**
2 **To Produce an Atmosphere of Warmth and Accept-ance**
3 **To Provide Sound Biblical Instruction**
4 **To Promote Daily Application of Biblical Material**

''I think, considering these objectives, that our next step should be deciding how best to organize our Sunday school classes to meet these objectives,'' Jim continued. ''Does everyone agree?''

It was unanimous. So the Taylors and Hamiltons finalized the time of the Tuesday night meeting, closed their Sunday school class with prayer, asking God to guide them in their upcoming meeting, and proceeded on to the worship service.

They had discovered that when a Sunday school knows where it is going, it is much easier to get there! And they were on their way!

FOOTNOTES

CHAPTER ONE

1 · 2 Corinthians 5:19, *New American Standard Bible.* © The Lockman Foundation, 1971. Used by permission.

2 · John 13:35.

3 · Kenneth S. Wuest, *Golden Nuggets from the Greek New Testament* (Grand Rapids: Wm. B. Eerdmans Publishing Company, 1940), p. 63.

4 · James 1:22, *King James Version.*

5 · James 2:17,20, *KJV.*

CHAPTER TWO

The King's Library

HOW DO WE GET WHERE WE'RE GOING?

"I really do believe you all mean business," laughed Tom Sanders, the Sunday school superintendent, "because you're all here on time!"

The Hamiltons and Taylors laughed too. "We do mean business, Tom. And that's why we asked you to join us. We want to help our Sunday school. We want it to be an effective tool for God. And that's why we're here. We'd like to get organized and get going."

"I'll be glad to help," Tom offered. "Why don't we start out by discussing adult organization in Sunday school?"

WHY ORGANIZE?

"We must answer this question," Tom said. "What organizational pattern and plan will be the most useful in helping us to reach the objectives of our Sunday school?"

"We've already listed the four objectives for adult Sunday school," Paul commented. "Let's go over them one more time."

1 To Reach Prospective Class members.

2 To Produce an Atmosphere of Warmth and Acceptance.

3 To Provide Sound Biblical Instruction.

4 To Promote Daily Application of Biblical Material.

"Do you agree with our conclusion that these are the four things we're trying to accomplish?"

"Absolutely! You four have done some good thinking on this," exclaimed Tom. "Now let's see why we must organize to achieve these objectives."

ORGANIZE TO INVOLVE

It should be remembered that organization is not an end in itself. It can be used, however, to better meet the needs of our learners. The first consideration in organizing adults is the need they have to most effectively be involved in the learning experiences which make up their Christian education. Learning is an active process; we all learn by doing. (Which is why correspondence courses in swimming have never been very successful.) A student must be encouraged to participate in, not just be a spectator of, the learning process. Maximum learning will not take place with minimum involvement, and this maximum involvement should extend beyond the classroom. Adults need to be actively involved with one another—in social activities, outreach efforts, and service projects associated with their Sunday school class. If they are, it will help meet the need for Christian fellowship. It will help each person feel that he is a participating member of the body of Christ throughout the week as well as on the Lord's Day. As a result of this continuing involvement outside of the classroom, relationships deepen and become more significant. Classroom interaction then becomes less superficial, and spiritual maturity is achieved more rapidly. So one of the first things to be considered is the importance of getting people deeply involved with the Word of God and with one another both in and outside of class.

"Well, there's an area we need to work on," volunteered Sandy. "Our class is only that—a class, with no outside involvement."

"Amen," chimed in Vicki. "Let's make that one of the first areas to organize."

ORGANIZE TO UNIFY

The second consideration to keep in mind in organizing adults is the importance of establishing a group of the recommended size. Trying to secure maximum involvement in too large a group often does nothing but frustrate everyone. It proves cumbersome, inefficient, and doesn't produce the desired results. There must be a definite limit to class size, and this will be discussed a bit later.

"Okay," said Tom. "Now we see why we need to get organized. But now we've got to decide who it is we're organizing. I suggest we tackle this next."

ORGANIZATIONAL GUIDELINES

Providing for maximum involvement and establishing individual classes of a size so that they can function properly are the goals of our organizational efforts. There are guidelines to help achieve these two things.

WHO IS AN ADULT?

In placing people together in an adult group, one of the first considerations is, "Who is an adult?" For the purposes of this book, an adult is a person who is eighteen years of age or older. Today eighteen year olds are accepting adult responsibilities in many areas. They have voting rights, serve in the armed forces, and an ever-increasing number of them are marrying and accepting the adult responsibilities of raising a family. Considering their role in our society, it is not inconsistent to categorize them as adults. But there are factors other than age which can serve as guidelines for grouping adults.

WHAT ARE HIS NEEDS?

The life needs which adults have must also be considered. These needs must be ministered to by relevantly applying the Word of God to adults' daily experiences. For example, scriptural principles of stewardship give guidelines for the use of time, money, and the abilities which God has given to each believer. Moreover, the

Word of God speaks on the issue of parent-child relationships. And biblical directives are given concerning employer-employee relationships. In a real sense the Word of God was designed by the Holy Spirit to speak to man where he is—in need of wisdom, guidance, and direction for living on a day-to-day basis. In this sense, adults are all in the same boat; there is a similarity of life needs among them.

"Now we have a two-dimensional guideline for grouping adults," Tom said. "They are:

1. Age
2. Life needs."

"Fine," said Jim. "But how do we organize all our adults into working units?"

"Ah, I thought you'd never ask!" Tom laughed. "There are several good reasons for grouping our adults into classes by their age. Let's talk about some of these reasons."

WHY GROUP BY AGE?

There is a place to start the process of grouping adults. In most cases, whether the church is large or small, it has been found that one of the most effective ways of grouping adults is by their age. Here are the three primary reasons for doing so.

EASILY ACCOUNTS FOR SIMILARITY OF NEEDS

First, there is a similarity of problems and needs among adults of the same general age level. To illustrate this, think of some individuals you know in their thirties. Isn't it true that they have similar interests with respect to marriage and family relationships, their stage of career development, and their physical health? Their interests in these three areas might be quite different from those held by people in the over-sixty-five age bracket. Age grouping tends to cluster together people who have similar needs and interests. And this helps in making teaching more effective and social exchanges and interaction more compatible.

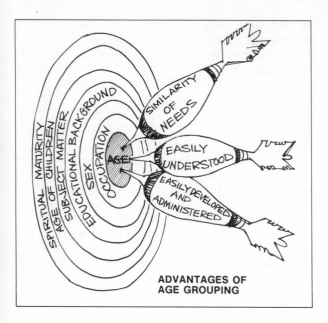

ADVANTAGES OF AGE GROUPING

SIMILARITY OF NEEDS

EASILY UNDERSTOOD

EASILY DEVELOPED AND ADMINISTERED

AGE

OCCUPATION

SEX

EDUCATIONAL BACKGROUND

SUBJECT MATTER

AGE OF CHILDREN

SPIRITUAL MATURITY

EASILY UNDERSTOOD BY PUPILS

The second advantage of age grouping is that it is easily understood by the participants. It is wonderfully inclusive. Everyone has an age and can therefore immediately determine in what group he belongs. There are only two possible difficulties that might be run into: (1) Some folks might not want to "fess up" to being a particular age, and (2) A married couple of different individual ages might find it difficult trying to decide which class to attend if they happened to find themselves "eligible" for two different age groups.

The second problem can be solved in one of two ways. Either the couple can choose which of the two groups they would rather be in or they can add up their two ages, divide by two, and take this average figure as the determining factor in deciding in which group they belong.

If a person is unwilling to "fess up" to his age, be sure he understands why he is being asked to attend a group of his own general age—to better meet the spiritual needs of all concerned. Appeal to his maturity and spirit of cooperation. If he is still unconvinced of the values of attending a particular class there is only one alternative: let him go where he will. It's better to have him in the "wrong" class than not in Sunday school at all!

EASILY DEVELOPED AND ADMINISTERED

A third advantage of age grouping is that it makes it easy to develop and administer an adult department or division. Not only is it a functional and workable way of dealing with the problem from the Sunday school administrator's standpoint. Everybody is included, because each person has an age classification. Visitors are quickly and easily placed into the proper group. The size of classes can be administratively controlled by decreasing the size of the age span when the class should be divided to form two new learning units. It is uncomplicated, and everyone can understand it.

"Let's stop a minute and get our bearings. We are grouping our adults according to age for three reasons," Tom summarized.

① It most efficiently and easily meets the needs of the pupils by putting them with others with similar problems and interests.

② It is a method that is easily understood by the pupils and therefore causes less confusion.

③ It is easily administered and developed by Sunday school leaders and provides a framework for adjusting to visitors and growing classes.

"This is great!" Paul exclaimed. "I feel like we're really making headway! Now we know why we need organization, how we determine what an adult is, and how we group our adults into classes."

"But I have a question," Sandy said. "How do we know that grouping by age is the best method? Aren't there other grouping methods that can be used?"

"That's a good question," commented Tom. "I think we need to understand why grouping by age works best. In order to understand this, why don't we take a look at some other methods and see what's disadvantageous about them."

INADEQUACIES OF OTHER GROUPING METHODS

There are a number of other ways in which adult grouping is being done in churches today. For instance, some churches group their adults on the basis of *sex:* they have classes for men and classes for women. *Individual interest* has been used as the basis for grouping by some churches. This would include such things as interest in the subject matter being taught, grouping people of similar occupations together, or those having children of the same age (or perhaps those having no children). Some churches have used educational background or similar hobbies as a basis for grouping people together. Sometimes people are allowed to choose the teacher they like. In this case grouping is based upon the *popularity of the teacher*. Other times, when given a choice, people attend a particular class because their *friends* do. Some churches attempt to group their adults on the basis of their *spiritual maturity*.

In theory, these popular bases for grouping sound pretty good. But in practice they fall short of the best. They create almost as many problems as they solve.

SEPARATION IS ARTIFICIAL

Separate classes for men and women have definite drawbacks. Class members need the benefit of the viewpoints held by members of the opposite sex, and keeping them separate creates an artificial situation. As such, it doesn't effectively equip people to live in the real world on Monday through Friday as well as some other means of grouping. If one were to insist on separate classes for men and women, it would be best to limit this to classes for the elderly, who may have lost their mates because of death.

SUBJECT IS TIME LIMITING

Grouping by subject matter is weak because of the time factor. When the course or subject matter is over, the class is disbanded. The things of Sunday school class life, such as the selection and installation of officers, is scarcely accomplished before it is time to start the process all over again with a new group of people.

OCCUPATION IS IMPRACTICAL

Grouping people by similar occupation often proves to be impractical because few churches have enough people of the same occupation (with the exception of housewives) to establish an effective class. How would numerical growth be initiated? (Would a class of lawyers invite and/or witness only to other lawyers?) The Great Commission is not that selective. People of different occupations need to mix and mingle together. It helps them personally and broadens their frame of reference so that they more effectively share their faith with unbelievers. This same question can be raised about grouping people on the basis of similar hobbies. Sunday school classes must be more than mutual admiration societies.

AGE OF CHILDREN IS UNWORKABLE

Grouping people on the basis of the age of children is not workable. Many families have college-age children as well as preschool ones. Which child's age determines the class that the parents attend? If they are allowed to pick which child they say will determine the class

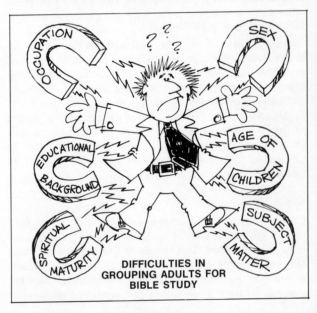

DIFFICULTIES IN GROUPING ADULTS FOR BIBLE STUDY

they will be in, what really is the basis for their grouping? It would appear that they are using some other factor to determine grouping (such as the teacher or the friends they may have in the class).

EDUCATIONAL BACKGROUND IS DIFFICULT

Similar educational background is not a particularly good way to group adults either. Again, it would create an artificial situation. We don't live life in a vacuum; we don't come in contact solely with people who have our particular educational background. And it would be difficult to solicit a class just for people with bachelor's degrees, master's degrees, or various doctoral degrees, perhaps having other classes for people who had not advanced formally beyond high school. This could result in the building of walls instead of bridges between people.

SPIRITUAL MATURITY IS UNSURE

Grouping adults on the basis of their spiritual maturity is probably the most difficult thing one could try. How is spiritual maturity determined? The amount of Bible knowledge one has is not a sure indication of spiritual maturity. Who is the judge of another's spiritual maturity?

"Wow, you've convinced me!" Jim exclaimed.

"Me too!" everyone else chimed in.

"Good," Tom smiled. "Now the next thing on our agenda is determining the size of the class—and why. Let's talk about that."

HOW BIG IS TOO BIG?

The position taken in this book is that the manageable size of an adult Sunday school class is 30 in attendance. The reasons for this number are given below.

30—A MANAGEABLE NUMBER

1 To promote a student-teacher relationship.
The first reason for suggesting that 30 is the recommended number for an adult class is because Sunday school is striving for educational soundness in its

classrooms. Although teaching methods and educational philosophy cannot be dealt with in depth in this organizational manual (see instead H. Norman Wright's *Ways to Help Them Learn: Adults),* a word must be said concerning this, because it does relate to how adults are organized.

An important factor in the learning process is the student-teacher relationship. When Sunday school is discussed, one is talking about a teacher ministering to the needs of students. One is talking about developing disciples of Jesus Christ. This goes far beyond the mere imparatation of knowledge. It means being open and honest and vulnerable—the sharing of a life. A familiar old poem expresses the importance of the student-teacher relationship.

> Mark Hopkins sat on one end of a log,
> A farm boy sat on the other.
> Mark Hopkins came as a pedagogue,
> And taught as an elder brother.
> I don't care what Mark Hopkins taught—
> If his Latin were crude and his Greek were naught.
> For the farmer's boy, he thought, thought he—
> All through lecture time and quiz—
> The kind of man I mean to be
> Is the kind of man Mark Hopkins is.

This poem helps to illustrate the fact that at any stage of maturity the student-teacher relationship is an important one. Limiting a class to 30 in number helps encourage a meaningful relationship between the teacher and the students.

2 To promote group interaction.
Person-to-person interaction is encouraged in a smaller group, and this is the second reason for maintaining 30 as a workable size for a Sunday school class. Sharing solutions to common problems can be a helpful thing in our classes. People are much more apt to share in a group of 30 than they are in a group of 60 or 90 or more.

People rarely interact with more than 30 others (if that many) in any given social activity. We gather and converse in relatively small groups. Yet 30 is a large enough number to insure everyone having fellowship. From a standpoint of the small number of people we relate to and converse with in a social situation, there isn't any need for having classes larger than 30.

3 To create a greater teaching variety.

Teaching methods such as buzz groups, discussion, and circle response can best be managed in the relatively small group of 30 in number. This size is a great help in promoting a greater variety of teaching methods and devices.

4 To promote leadership.

The fourth reason for limiting adult class sizes to 30 is to provide sufficient leadership for future growth and outreach. If a large class of 90 is divided into three classes of 30 each, three times as many teachers will be needed. With leadership at a premium in most churches, it may seem as if this is defeating the purpose by creating the need for additional class officers and teachers. But smaller class size makes the recruitment of teachers and leaders easier. Many people who may feel unqualified to teach a group of 90 or 100 might "give it a try" with a smaller group. In this way, leadership is allowed to emerge; consequently, it is possible to have more leaders recruited, trained, and developed.

5 To facilitate administration.

Fifth, this size of 30 takes into account the administration concept of a ratio of five to one of followers to leader. This concept will be discussed below and explained further. But a class size of 30 allows the class to be divided into workable units of follow-up, outreach, and social activity.

"Wow," said Jim. "You've convinced me that a class should be no bigger than 30 pupils in attendance."

"Good," answered Tom. "But let's review the reasons for this once more so that we can have them firmly in our minds."

WHY 30 IS THE RECOMMENDED CLASS SIZE

(1) It helps achieve a beneficial teacher-student relationship.

(2) It encourages and promotes sufficient group interaction.

(3) It allows for a greater variety of teaching methods.

4. It encourages and promotes leadership.
5. It is easily administered by the units which are created within the class.

"Here's a concept we need to understand in order to help our classes realize their potential," Tom added. "It's called 'span of control.'"

SPAN OF CONTROL

Picture in your mind's eye a typical organizational chart. It looks something like this:

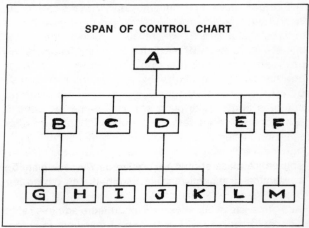

SPAN OF CONTROL CHART

Notice that person "B" has 2 people ("G" and "H") who are responsible to him and for whom he is responsible. Persons "E" and "F" each have 1 ("L" and "M," respectively). Person "D" has 3 people ("I," "J," and "K") who, in a sense, work for him. Person "A" has the largest number on his staff (persons "B" through "F").

Look at the chart again. Person "B" has 2 people reporting to him—or a "span of control" of 2. Persons "E" and "F" each have a span of control of 1. How large is person "D's" span of control? (If you said 3, you're right! Keep this up and you'll graduate with honors!) Person "A" has a span of control of 5. Persons "A," "B," "D," "E," and "F" administratively (not *dictatorially*) control the people directly below them on the chart. All that this means is that the responsibility for the operation of the organization has been divided up and delegated to other people. If a problem arises in person "L's" department, chief executive "A" simply talks to person "E" and helps him solve the problem. So it can be seen that span of control simply refers to the number of individuals reporting or responsible to any one leader or officer.

From the standpoint of organizational efficiency, no one person should have more than 5 or 6 people directly responsible to him.

"Well, this is all very interesting," Vicki said, "but what does it have to do with our Sunday school class?"

"Glad you asked," Tom smiled. "Now we're going to talk about an effective way to keep those 30 people in our class tuned in to each other and aware of their position in the class as a whole."

"You give me the answer to that 'problem'," Jim commented, "and it will solve half the problems in my Sunday school class."

CLASS UNITS

The entire class should recognize its responsibility for contacting prospective class members. This outreach can be made more effective by organizing and administering the efforts of the class as a whole. The responsibility for coordinating the class's outreach efforts should be delegated to an individual. The logical person to fill this role would be the class president. To emphasize his leadership role, it would be well to designate his title as that of "class leader"—one of his major responsibilities being to lead and coordinate the entire class in contacting prospects.

One of the most efficient ways for him to do this would be to divide the class into groups or units. Remembering the span of control ratio of 5 or 6 to 1, the class of 30 is best divided up into 5 units. This would result in the 5 units having about 6 members each. (Or this could be 6 couples, which would give even fewer units. The unit leaders would have greater responsibility, the class leader less. It might be more efficient this way.)

Since it is best for the class leader to have only 5 or 6 people and not 30 people reporting to him, it is clear that each of the 5 units would have to have one of its members function as the unit leader. The person filling this role would have the other 5 or 6 members responsible to him. So, limiting the class size to 30 in number allows us to organize the class's outreach efforts utilizing the span of control ratio of 5 or 6 to 1 on all levels. Organizational chart on page 40 may help to clarify this.

MAXIMUM CLASS SIZE

It has been stated that the recommended class size is 30. What happens when our outreach efforts prove effective and new people join our class? How do we handle this numerical growth? Is there a maximum size to which we should limit our classes? Yes, there is. When the class reaches 40 in attendance, it is time to create a new learning unit. The group of 40 should be divided into two groups of 20 each. When these two new groups each reach 40, they should in turn divide into two groups of 20 each. It is surprising how rapidly numerical growth can take place with everyone doing his part in the matter of outreach.

HOW SMALL IS TOO SMALL?

It should be recognized that for many churches classes of 30 in number are in the future. Rather than maximum size, they may be struggling with the question of minimum size. Can one have an effective class with just 1 or 2 people in it? Most certainly the process of discipleship can work on a one-to-one basis. But as a general rule, the minimum effective number for an adult class would be 5 members. The learners plus the teacher would form one outreach unit themselves, and motivation for growth would be high. Less than that number often tends to be discouraging.

"I'm getting so excited!" Sandy exclaimed. "I can't wait to put all this into action!"

"Wait. There's more!" Tom commented. "We haven't even talked about curriculum yet. Or putting our efforts into actually organizing the adult division. First let's talk about the kind of curriculum the adult Sunday school can best use."

THIS ORGANIZATION PLAN IS FLEXIBLE

The "limit-divide-grow" concept that is being suggested in this book will work whether a Sunday school is utilizing a uniform lesson plan (all adult classes studying the same lesson materials), an individual class lesson plan (each class studying a lesson which differs from that studied by other classes), or an elective class plan (entire classes or individuals within classes choosing a particular course of study from several different ones being offered simultaneously).

If plan 3 (an elective class plan) is used, the class in which a particular student is a permanent member becomes the "home base" out of which he may go to another location for class study time. When using this elective system, it is often more effective to have the class study period first and then move to the "home base" classes for a closing assembly time. Here's why:

1 By meeting after the teaching period, the last association a person has is with his "home base" class. He would then leave Sunday school with a sense of belonging and a sense of identity with a specific group of people. Perhaps he is better acquainted with these people than he is with any other group in the church.

2 The fellowship time allows for a break between the class study period and the worship service. The student would then be better prepared for a more meaningful worship experience.

3 New people are more easily integrated into the home base class. They come back after the study time, which means that the unit leaders don't have to search frantically for the visitors who have scattered to the elective classes.

"One of the strengths of age grouping," Tom informed his listeners, "is its inherent flexibility. It can be used successfully with any type of curriculum system and it will enable our adult Sunday school classes to make significant progress in achieving the four objectives of Sunday school."

"I agree," chimed in Jim. "Now show us how to carry out this organizational grouping in our adult Sunday school!"

READY ... SET ... GO!

"Okay," Tom answered. "We know now that the recommended class size is 30. We know that grouping by age is the most effective method in our adult Sunday school. We understand the span of control concept of 5 to 1. Let's take an example and see how to break it down into working groups."

GROUP YOUR ADULTS

The best place to start is by placing the adults into three groups: Young Adults (18 to 35), Middle-Aged Adults (36 to 59), and Older Adults (60 and above).

However, collegians seem to have unique characteristics and needs. For this reason, it is advantageous to have a separate class for them. Single adults are also helped by having a separate class—age grouped, of course, if there are that many.

Probably the easiest way to do this is to take an anonymous "age poll" of your adults. It can be as simple as passing out a three-by-five card to each person on which he is to put his age and marital status. These cards should be collected and kept as a source of age distribution information which can be used in establishing the number of classes.

ANALYZE AGE DISTRIBUTION

The second step is to analyze the age distribution within each of these three large age groupings. They will need to be divided further because, ideally, there should not be a wider age span than 10 to 15 years in any group of adults. If this principle must be bent, however, it is most easily bent in the over-60 age bracket.

Thus in a group of adults aged 18 and older, you might wish to incorporate these age groupings: 18 to 24 (college age), 25 to 35, 36 to 49, 50 to 59, and 60 and above.

SEPARATE BY AGE

Now let's put it all together and see how this will work in actual practice. Let's assume for the purpose of illustration that there is an adult division in a Sunday school and it is comprised of 100 individuals.

Step 1: Gather the age distribution cards. After they are collated, the following age distribution has been arrived at: 33 people are Young Adults (age 18 to 35); there are 59 Middle Adults (age 36 to 59); and there are 8 Older Adults (age 60 and above).

Step 2: Analyze the distribution within each of these larger age distributions. In so doing, it is discovered that 9 of the Young Adults are college age and 24 are not. Of these 24, 7 are single. Because of the unique needs of collegians and singles, it is best to have a separate class for each of them. Thus, there would be three Young Adult classes: 9 pupils in a college age class, 7 in a singles class, and 17 in a young marrieds class, (a woman may attend Sunday school without her husband, or one partner may be teaching in another age group).

The analysis of the Middle Adults reveals that of the total number of 59, 25 are in the 36 to 39 bracket, 15 are in the 40 to 49 bracket, and 19 people are in the 50 to 59 age division. This leaves 8 individuals in the 60 and above bracket.

CREATE ADULT CLASSES

Thus, with 100 individuals distributed as above, we would have 7 adult classes grouped in the following manner:

Young Adults	
College Age	9
Singles (25-35)	7
Marrieds (18-35)	17
Middle Adults	
Age 36 to 39	25
Age 40 to 49	15
Age 50 to 59	19
Older Adults	
Age 60 and over	8
Total	100

Tom's four "pupils" were on the edge of their chairs as he finished. "Well, that's how to organize an adult Sunday school," he said, leaning back into the cushion of the couch.

"Great!" Paul exclaimed.

"Sensational!" Vicki agreed.

"Let's get going on it right away!" Jim urged.

Tom lifted up his hand. "Wait a minute," he said. "We still have a lot more to learn."

"You mean there's more?" Sandy asked, wide-eyed.

"Much more. What about your leaders and officers? What do they do? How do they do it? What about equipment? The classroom environment? How and when do your teachers meet and plan their lessons? These things don't just happen, you know. We have to plan for them in order to make the most effective use of our Sunday school."

"Okay," Jim spoke up. "Let's meet at my house next week. Same time, same subject. We'll listen to what you have to say again, Tom, if that's all right with you."

Tom smiled. "I've never had such a willing audience. It's a deal!"

CHAPTER THREE

WHO'S GOING TO LEAD US?

The following week, the Hamiltons, the Taylors, and Tom Sanders met again. Tom came with a notebook filled with papers and notes he had taken in seminars on Sunday school.

"Tonight we're going to talk about class leaders," he told the listening group. "We'll find out what each leader does and how. By the end of the evening, you'll know the responsibilities of each class officer."

"I feel like we're in school," Jim smiled. "And it's a great education. Tom, we really want to thank you for taking the time to meet with us like this. I know you're busy."

"My pleasure," Tom answered. "It's always exciting for me to find people who are interested in improving their Sunday school. Why don't we begin with the teacher and discuss his job."

THE BIBLE TEACHER

The first class leader is the Bible teacher. It is unfortunate that in some churches the teacher is sort of an outsider. He comes in Sunday morning, ministers, and goes on his way with little if any further relationship to the class members. But he should be like other class members—a part of the class whose involvement is more

than just on Sundays. He is not an "ivory tower" man but an integral part of the class.

1 The teacher works in close cooperation with the other class leaders so that he and they feel a part of the "team."

2 One of the teacher's most important functions is to guide the learners in their discovery of biblical truth. Much of today's teaching emphasizes what the teacher does—rather than what the student does—in the process of learning. The lecture method is often overused and rarely used effectively by an individual. Consequently, the image many people have of adult Sunday school is something rather unexciting—if not actually boring.

But if the teacher realizes that he is to guide the students in *their* discovery of biblical truth, exciting changes will take place. The old adage of "You sit still while I instill" must be replaced by a better one: "Never tell a pupil anything he is capable of discovering for himself." As the teacher guides the pupils in learning, he is free to use new and creative teaching methods.[1]

3 As he guides his students, the teacher should also be a helpful resource person. He should feel free to suggest ways in which the biblical truth discovered in class may be expressed in concrete ways both inside and outside the classroom.

"Wow," exclaimed Jim, "that's a tall order to fill! But you know something? I'm glad I know now exactly what I *am* supposed to be doing. It's better than stumbling around in the dark and not being sure of myself."

God has not left us to our own devices. He never calls us to a position of service without equipping us for the task.

"I realize," Tom continued, "that our meeting here tonight is not primarily for the purpose of Bible study. But let's take a couple of minutes and look at the Scriptures concerning the gifts of the Holy Spirit which God gives to His people so that they can serve Him effectively.

"Turn to Romans 12. I want to read the sixth verse from *The Living Bible:* 'God has given each of us the ability to do certain things well.' Paul then states in the seventh verse that teachers should do a good job of teaching. Paul lists the other gifts of the Holy Spirit in this chapter, but we won't deal with these right now."

"When can we?" Sandy interrupted. "I want to know more about the gifts of the Holy Spirit! Every Christian has one, right?"

"Yes," replied Tom, "every Christian has at least one gift of the Holy Spirit. But we will digress from our immediate concern if we start discussing this subject. We'd be here all night! During this week check out I Corinthians 12, Romans 12 and Ephesians 4. It might be a good topic for discussion at our next class social.

"But here's the point we need to remember. It is absolutely essential that the teacher have the proper gift of the Holy Spirit—the gift of teaching. Christians are to serve God by using the gift of the Holy Spirit that He has imparted to them.

"A teacher must be equipped *by* God. And he also must be committed *to* God; his life should be characterized by actively seeking to let Jesus Christ be the Lord of all of his life. All known sin should be confessed and forsaken.

"All of us here in this room know that this should be true of all Christians, not just Sunday school teachers. But it needs to be stressed that serving God in general, and teaching Sunday school in specific, is a ministry—a spiritual, not a mechanical, endeavor. God equips us and empowers us to serve Him. We're not in there alone.

"And humanly speaking *you're* not in there by yourself either, Jim," Tom reminded him. "The other class officers are there to help you and make the class run more smoothly. Let's look at the class leader."

THE CLASS LEADER

The second class officer is the class leader. Although his role includes that of the traditional class president, it also goes beyond that.

1 The class leader is the primary administrator of the class. Under his direction the class does its part in achieving the four objectives of the Sunday school.

2 He helps to keep the class "people-oriented" by working closely with the unit leaders in contacting and

cultivating prospective class members.

3 He shares planning responsibilities with the teacher for coordinating the entire class session.

4 He is the primary channel of communication between the Sunday school's administrative staff and the individual class.

5 As class administrator, he interprets the job descriptions for the other class leaders.

"Hey," Jim spoke up, "I think I know a good man for this job!" He smiled at Paul with a gleam in his eye.

"Oh, oh," Paul laughed, "get the teacher excited and he goes wild recommending leadership!"

They all laughed. Tom looked down at his notes and interrupted the laughter. "Onward," he said.

THE CLASS SECRETARY

The third position of class leadership is that of the class secretary.

1 The class secretary is responsible for any clerical work associated with the class's ministry. He works in close cooperation with the other class officers—the teacher, the class leader, the unit leaders, and the social chairman.

2 He maintains a prospect file on potential members. This is not to suggest that he is the only one who comes up with names of prospective members. But he does act as a clearing house for all the names given to him by the unit leaders and then coordinates with the class leader in implementing the class's visitation program.

3 He maintains a class membership list. This is readily available to the other class leaders to be used as a mailing list.

4 The class secretary takes minutes at the class business meetings. He also handles finances for both in-class and out-of-class activities. Each class, of course, does not need its own bank account or funding system, but the class secretary is to see that the Sunday school offering is given to the proper person or taken to the proper place. Or if there were ticket sales in conjunction with a class social, the class secretary, in coordination

with the social chairman, would be in charge of this. It is a matter of efficiency to have one person in charge of anything having to do with money; the class secretary is the logical one to assume this task.

"I like that job," Vicki said with a gleam in her eye and rubbing her hands together, "getting to keep charge of all that money!"

"It seems to me," Paul added, "that the class secretary has an important job. I always thought he just took roll and that was it."

"I think we're beginning to see that the class leaders are very vital in the Sunday school ministry," Tom commented. "Here's another officer whose role is extremely significant."

THE UNIT LEADER

The class unit leader is the fourth position of leadership.

1 A unit leader functions as sort of an undershepherd. The members of his unit are his flock. This concept should be clarified. The unit leader is not in competition with the pastor. The terms *undershepherd* and *flock* when applied to the unit leader refer to attitude, not office. He is concerned and cares for the members in his unit. He encourages regular attendance in Sunday school and church services and urges his unit members to cultivate prospective class members.

The pastor should feel a sense of relief in knowing that there are other people who have genuine concern for members in the adult Sunday school classes. And as the unit leader ministers to his unit members, he should be sensitive to problems needing pastoral care. When he becomes aware of such problems, he should quickly alert the pastor concerning these needs.

2 The unit leader functions as a channel of communication, motivation, and activation between the class leader and the unit members. The class leader looks to him to involve his unit members in class service projects and social activities.

3 When a new person begins attending the Sunday school class, he is placed into a unit. The unit leader

does everything that he can to make the new person feel welcome and a part of the group. He makes sure the newcomer is introduced to the other unit members, as well as to the other class members. (That is, those who are members of other units—everyone in the class belongs to a unit.) At class social functions the unit leader makes sure that any newcomers to his unit are integrated into the larger group.

4 On Sunday mornings and at out-of-class activities the unit leader makes a mental note of who in his unit is absent. He then follows up on these absentees and lets them know they were missed. He is vital in making people feel wanted and accepted in the group.

"That's a big responsibility! The unit leader will have to be someone who really cares about people," Sandy commented.

"Right," Tom agreed. "All class leaders—and members—should care about people. But there's one more officer. Let's find out about him."

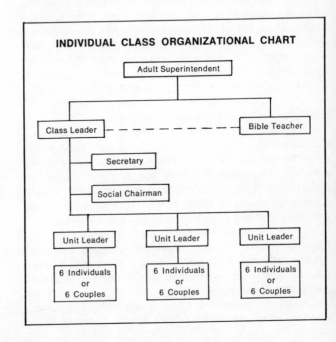

INDIVIDUAL CLASS ORGANIZATIONAL CHART

THE SOCIAL CHAIRMAN

The fifth and last class leader is the social chairman.

1 The social chairman, who is directly responsible to the class leader, provides the leadership in planning social activities for the entire class. These social activities should take place on a regular basis—perhaps monthly.

Note that this person is to provide the leadership in planning—not do all of the work! It simply means that he makes sure that all of the bases are covered with regard to the detailed plans. He should delegate much of the responsibility to other class members. This not only gives them a ministry to the rest of the class but also illustrates the fact that each class member plays an important role in helping to achieve the four objectives of the adult Sunday school. (The planning guide on page 102 will help the social chairman in his ministry to the class.)

2 It has been stated that one of the reasons for limiting the size of an adult class is to assure maximum involvement of the members for both in-class and out-of-class activities. The social chairman should plan for ways in which each person can be actively involved in the social functions. The class social times should be structured so that members and visitors have the opportunity to get to know one another. Class socials should be a time of deepening interpersonal relationships.

"There you have it, gang," Tom said, smiling. "These are the five positions of leadership in an adult Sunday school class: the Bible teacher, the class leader, the class secretary, the unit leader, and the social chairman. Here's a chart (page 40) which shows how these leaders relate to one another organizationally. When these five people are working together, you can be sure that the Sunday school class will be running at maximum efficiency."

"It's a real challenge," Jim mused. "But I'm more excited than ever about teaching the Young Marrieds class now. With a little help from my friends, the other class officers, we should be able to turn people on to this class!"

"Pretty soon your class will be so big you won't know how to manage it," Tom said.

"Wow! Would I like to have that problem!"

"One day you might," Tom cautioned. "That's why I suggest we discuss organizing departments and divisions next week—before growth can become a problem."

"I'll second that," Paul agreed. "I'm really looking forward to these weekly meetings now. I feel like we're really accomplishing something productive."

FOOTNOTE

CHAPTER THREE

1 · H. Norman Wright, *Ways to Help Them Learn: Adults* (Glendale, Calif.: G/L Publications, 1971).

CHAPTER FOUR

WHAT HAPPENS WHEN WE GROW?

The following week, the Taylors, Hamiltons, and Tom met again. This evening, Tom's wife Linda joined them. She too was interested in helping to build up the adult Sunday school in their church.

"Looks like we'll have the whole Sunday school meeting with us before we're through!" Jim commented.

"We've got an important subject on our hands tonight, folks. We've talked about the individual classes and how to organize them. But if we go no further than this, that is all they will ever be: individual classes which will tend to become isolated units. When this happens, they feel unrelated to the church as a whole. A feeling of abandonment, of being left without resources and help in dealing with class problems, may permeate the class leadership, and when this happens, serving Christ in a position of leadership becomes a burden instead of a joy."

"I know that feeling well, Tom," Jim interjected, "and I'm anxious to learn how to solve it."

"There are other problems as well," Tom went on. " 'Quality control' can become a problem when individual classes are left to function on their own. Some classes may work wonderfully well with the members enthusiastic about what is taking place in their particular Sunday school class.

"But what about those classes that are unable to function as well? Perhaps their leaders are not as experienced as those of the better-functioning classes. Perhaps the Bible teacher is not as well trained or as experienced. Any number of factors may cause a difference between two classes. The quality of the teaching/learning experience may vary enough from one independent class to another as to create dissatisfaction on the part of entire classes.

"Or another problem can be that of independent classes becoming ingrown. This will unravel much of the work we have already done, because people will find it difficult to graduate up to the next age group. Consequently, our age grouping disintegrates and we will not be able to achieve the original purpose of age grouping; to better meet the needs of the individual students."

"Wow, that's a lot of problems!" Paul exclaimed. "Is there any way to circumvent them in our Sunday school?"

"You bet!" Tom enthused. "We can create an adult department for our Sunday school."

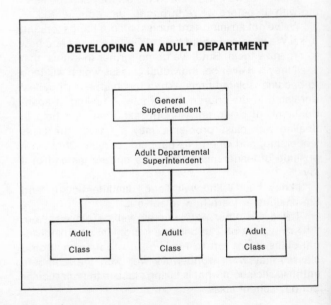

DEVELOPING AN ADULT DEPARTMENT

General Superintendent

Adult Departmental Superintendent

Adult Class   Adult Class   Adult Class

BENEFITS OF AN ADULT DEPARTMENT

"Let's look at some of the values of organizing our adult Sunday school classes into an adult department," Tom said.

RELATES ADULTS TO THE ENTIRE CHURCH

First, departmentalization relates each individual class to the rest of the church. It helps to create and maintain an esprit de corps between the adults and the rest of the Sunday school.

INCREASES HELP

A second value is that the class officers have other people to help them in their ministries to their classes. Who are these people? The adult department superintendent is a very important person to give aid and assistance, as well as class leaders from other adult classes. The leaders should meet regularly with the department superintendent. These meetings can be used to tackle problems and to share solutions that have proved workable in other classes. Such subjects as effective teaching procedures, means of outreach, ideas for socials, ways of caring for class members—would be shared at these meetings. In this way the classes help one another to be successful. This pooling of creative thought is of great encouragement to those who are having difficulties and helps assure a measure of quality control throughout the adult classes.

INCREASES MOTIVATION

In the third place, departmentalizing our adults is helpful in keeping them motivated and activated. The entire department can take on a service project that is too large for an individual class. Quarterly socials for the entire department can give everyone the feeling of being successful because larger numbers of people are present. Along this line, attendance drives are often more effective when approached by the whole department. Under the guidance of an adult department, a complete program for the members can be provided.

IMPROVES LEADERSHIP

Better leadership development is a fourth advantage to departmentalizing adults. Training courses offered for adult leaders can be more efficiently administered on the department level instead of for each individual class.

Inexperienced class leaders can benefit greatly from the departmental meeting with the more seasoned leaders, and the department superintendent is available to give aid and assistance to class leaders. Recruiting new class leaders is easier because they know that they won't be left to flounder on their own. The department superintendent and the leaders from the other classes are there to help the new recruits in their ministry.

MAINTAINS AGE GROUPING

Lastly, departmentalization of adults encourages the maintenance of age grouping and the graduation or promotion of people from one age group into another. By doing things on a department-wide basis, the people in other classes are not strangers to one another. Department socials, department witness or visitation projects, or service projects familiarize all the adults with one another. When it comes time for them to move up to the next age grouped class, they won't feel that they are being thrust into a group of strangers.

"I'm convinced that a Sunday school adult department has many advantages," Jim said. "But how do we know when we need one in our church? I mean, if there is only one adult class, for example, do we need a department?"

"Good question," Tom responded. "If there is only one adult class, that class would, in effect, be its own department. But if we have more than one class, there are several criteria which determine when a department should be created."

WHEN TO CREATE AN ADULT DEPARTMENT

At what point in a Sunday school's development is it necessary to think in terms of organizing an adult department?

NUMBER OF ADULTS

The answer to this question depends upon the number of adults in the Sunday school program. If there is only one adult class, an adult department is not needed. In effect, that one class is its own department. But the existence of two adult Sunday school classes justifies organizing them into an adult department.

AVAILABILITY OF LEADERSHIP

A second criterion for inaugurating an adult department is the available leadership which will be needed. A department superintendent will be necessary, since the general superintendent of the Sunday school cannot possibly maintain the type of involvement that is necessary for the adult department and carry on his other duties as well.

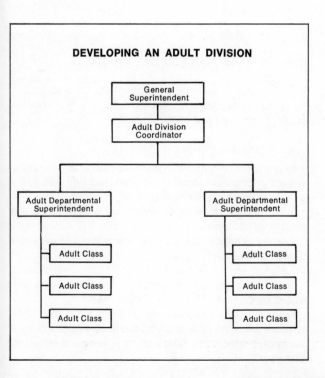

DEVELOPING AN ADULT DIVISION

WHEN TO CREATE AN ADULT DIVISION

Two adult classes require organization into an adult department. When the adult department grows to five classes, it is time to organize them into two adult departments. (See chart on page 47.) Two or more adult departments make up the adult division, and each department requires two adult department superintendents.

An adult division is needed, therefore, when there are two or more adult departments.

"If our Sunday school starts growing, we may need a department and then a division in the near future," Paul commented.

"Now that's what I like—a man with a vision!" Tom responded enthusiastically. "And the bigger you get, the more leadership you need. So let's look at some of the people who make a department and a division function effectively."

LEADERS IN THE ADULT SUNDAY SCHOOL

When an adult department is created, there is a need for a superintendent, since he will help to maintain the span of control ratio of five to one.

THE DEPARTMENT SUPERINTENDENT

The department superintendent's position is not just to keep our organizational chart neat and tidy. He has a very important ministry.

1 He discovers, recommends, and enlists personnel for the adult department.

2 He guides the class leaders and Bible teachers in their ministries and is a channel of communication from the higher administrative levels to the individual classes.

3 He takes the lead in securing proper facilities and equipment.

4 He projects future needs in the school which will result from numerical growth, such as additional adult classroom space, teaching aids, songbooks, and bulletin boards.

5 He is the adult department representative on the Sunday School Council. This council, which should meet monthly under the direction of the general Sunday school superintendent, makes plans for the future of the Sunday school and resolves existing problems in the school.

6 The adult department superintendent guides in the development of what may be called "away from church" ministries for shut-ins, the hospitalized, and those who are unable to attend on Sunday for any reason.

7 The adult department superintendent also assists the individual classes in developing their visitation program.

8 He is a link between class members and the rest of the Sunday school. Class members need to be aware of the superintendent's ministry. This means that the superintendent needs to be involved with the classes in some way on Sunday morning.

It may be as simple as having him make announcements which are of significance to the department as a whole on Sunday morning, such as attendance drives or department socials. He is the person who links the adults to the rest of the Sunday school. Individual classes should feel free to invite him to their functions. It would not be out of order, if a brief devotional message is part of an evening's social program, to have the adult department superintendent bring such a message occasionally.

THE DIVISION COORDINATOR

When there is a need for several department superintendents, the number of people reporting to the general superintendent of the Sunday school is multiplied. This defeats one of the purposes of maintaining the span of control ratio, since the general superintendent then would become responsible for more than five people. So an additional person is needed to function as an adult division coordinator.

1 The adult department superintendents are directly responsible to the division coordinator. He, in turn, is then responsible to the general superintendent.

2 The adult division coordinator guides the adult de-

partment superintendents in their ministries and cooperates with the general superintendent in discovering, securing, and recommending personnel.

3 He also works closely with the general superintendent in planning and evaluating the work of the adult division.

"There you have it!" Tom finished. "Those are the people who help make the Sunday school work effectively as it grows."

"That should be a worthwhile goal for us," Jim interjected. "We ought to be working toward the day when we'll need an adult division coordinator in our Sunday school!"

"That is a worthwhile goal," Tom said, "but first we need to be sure that these leaders know what they're doing. A lot of leaders all running around not knowing their tasks doesn't make a good Sunday school. So we need to be meeting together regularly as Sunday school leaders to plan and evaluate all that we're doing. I think that will be our topic for next week. The weekly 'Sunday school organizing committee' is hereby adjourned."

"Not so fast," Vicki stood up. "I've got coffee and cake in the other room!"

"Who said organizing Sunday school was no fun?" Paul asked, smiling.

"It's interesting *and* fun," Sandy commented. "And high in calories!"

school organizing committee, as Hetty Ackley said.
Not so fast." Vicki stood up. "Five and noise

HOW DO WE KEEP IT GOING?

"The meeting will come to order!" Tom Sanders said, hitting his loafer on the top of the coffee table. "I don't mean to rush things, but we have a lot of material to cover."

"We're ready," Jim agreed. "Shoot."

"How many of you have ever attended a Sunday school planned meeting?" Tom asked.

"I did—once—when I took the job as the Young Marrieds teacher," Jim volunteered.

No one else spoke up.

"I assume the rest of you haven't been at a meeting to plan for Sunday school?"

Four heads shook. "They sound awfully dull to me," Sandy said.

"It's too bad that you have that conception of planning meetings, Sandy. Because they are a vital part of our Sunday school and can make it into the organization we want it to be."

"I must admit I sure could use some help in planning my class," Jim commented.

"And that's what these meetings are all about," Tom said. "If we can meet with our Sunday school staff on a regular basis, each person can help the others and receive help in turn. And in that way, we can improve our Sunday school continuously. Let's look at how this is done."

WHY MEET?

In the fourth chapter of Ephesians Paul tells us the purpose for which God has gifted individuals in the church: "for the equipping of the saints for the work of service, to the building up of the body of Christ."[1] Recognizing that "saints" is a New Testament synonym for a believer in Jesus Christ, it is evident that an important task for leaders in the local church is to equip fellow believers for successful ministering work.

In order to equip people to minister effectively, time must be spent with them—but not just to be with them and hope that they will "pick up" how to get their job done. Meaningful training opportunities must be provided for these people by meeting and sharing with them on a regularly scheduled basis. These meetings must be well planned. The various classes and leaders in the adult department or division need to feel a part of the whole with an esprit de corps among them.

MONTHLY CONFERENCES

Many churches have found that an effective way to do this is to conduct a monthly planning meeting or workers conference. These conferences are strategic because in them leaders can plan what is going to happen during the Sunday school hour and in related activities.

Too often teachers are left on their own with little or no communication between them and the class leader. The result is that the teacher walks in Sunday morning to do his "teacher thing" with no one except him knowing what is going to take place next. The opening assembly time has no relationship to the Bible lesson under these circumstances, and the "preliminaries," it is felt, must be hurried along so that the class can get to the Bible lesson.

There is a better way. By planning together there can be meaningful correlation between the Bible lesson and the opening assembly time. There can also be common understanding and mutual support of one another concerning such things as attendance goals, the overall

Sunday school calendar, help in recruiting people for training classes, and the coordination of any changes that may need to be made regarding the physical setup of the rooms. The values of monthly planning meetings are many, and the returns well worth the effort of conducting them.

"How do we do it?" is the next question which must be answered. Here is a plan that gets the job done in many churches. This concept of a monthly workers conference or planning meeting is most easily grasped by thinking of it as taking place in three time modules.

FIRST TIME MODULE

The first time module is from 7:00 to 7:30. During this period the Sunday School Council meets. This group is comprised of the following individuals: (1) the general superintendent, (2) the department superintendents, and (3) the division coordinators, if there are any.

Here are the activities which take place during this first time module:

1 Discussion of the overall calendar. Nailing down of dates which affect the entire school, such as the dates for the annual picnic, the March-to-Sunday-School-in-March attendance campaign, the Christmas program, the Fall Workers Appreciation Banquet, etc.

2 Discussion of problem areas. Is additional personnel needed? Where? Are any changes needed in the physical setup of the rooms? Do some of the age-grouped classes need to exchange places because a class in a smaller room is growing numerically faster than a class in a larger room?

3 Communication and formulation of plans for the second time module, the general session. What will the agenda be for the second time module? What is going to be discussed which the leadership needs to be alerted to so that they can make specific application of it to their individual department or class?

Once again, those participating in the first time module, the general council, are:

> the general Sunday school superintendent
> the department superintendents
> the division coordinators (if any)

SECOND TIME MODULE

The second time module or general session could run from 7:30 to 8:00. All Sunday school personnel—superintendents, teachers, secretaries, and the adult class unit leaders—should be present. These are the kinds of activities which will take place during the general session:

1 The communication of information concerning the overall calendar of events which affect the entire school.

2 There might be a brief inspirational talk by the pastor or some other leader.

3 General motivation for more effective teaching, visitation, etc.

Once again, those attending the second time module are:

> the general Sunday school superintendent
> the department superintendents
> the division coordinators (if any)
> all teachers
> all class secretaries
> all adult class unit leaders

THIRD TIME MODULE

The third time module, the departmental sessions, will last about an hour—from 8:00 to 9:00. During this last session there are three primary activities:

1 The specific application and/or interpretation of the information communicated in the general session. For instance, if a March-to-Sunday-School-in-March campaign has been announced, in what way will the adults in particular participate in this? Or if an all-Sunday school visitation night has been announced in the general session, the mechanics of adult participation in this will need to be discussed.

2 The discussion and implementation of details concerning the care of the adult enrollment. Is outreach being done effectively? Is follow-up of absentees efficient? What can be done to improve it? Is there adequate communication concerning the social activities of the various classes? Are visitors made aware of up-and-coming social activities?

3 Teaching improvement. Time in this third module can be profitably spent in answering the question, "What are we going to teach on Sunday morning for the next several weeks?" Curricula are usually set up in units of study; normally three to five lessons comprise a unit. Such a group of lessons have a similar purpose. A unit is more like one continuing lesson three to five Sundays long than three to five isolated lessons. Each lesson of the unit is planned and taught with this in mind. Planning for each unit in the curriculum can be handled on a monthly basis during the departmental meeting.

4 If your adult department or division is on a uniform lesson plan (that is, all adult classes studying the same lesson), this time can be spent in determining what teaching methods will be employed in the different sessions comprising the unit. Perhaps it would be advantageous to have the "opening assembly" time later in the hour; it could well be that some teaching time prior to the so-called preliminaries will make the hymns which are sung at that time more meaningful. These kinds of things are best planned a unit at a time. It should be a team effort of the superintendent, teachers, and class leaders.

5 If your adult department or division is on an elective system (that is, each class studying a different lesson), then the third module is best spent discussing effective ways of teaching adults. (See H. Norman Wright's book entitled, *Ways to Help Them Learn: Adults.*) The individual teachers would then do unit planning for the class session on a one-to-one basis with his class leader.

Graphically these monthly workers conferences can be represented by the chart on the following page.

WEEKLY MEETINGS

Some churches have found it advantageous to hold the departmental meetings on a weekly basis. The emphasis is then on specific lesson plans rather than the broader unit planning. This is the equivalent of the third time module, meeting instead on a weekly basis.

PLANNING MEETING FORMAT		
MODULE		
Sunday School Council	Entire Staff (or Adult Division)	Department Sessions
Discussion of overall calendar	Communication of overall calendar events	Specific application and/or interpretation of information communicated in General Session
Discussion of problem areas	Brief inspirational talk	Discussion of details of the "caring" ministry of the adult enrollment
Communication and formulation of plans for second time module	General motivation for more effective teaching, visitation, etc.	Teaching improvement: lesson unit planning and/or planning for specific teaching methods to be used

CLASS LEADER MEETINGS

A word needs to be said concerning one other type of meeting involving all of the class leaders. A time is definitely needed when the class leaders, which includes the teacher, the secretary, the class leader, the unit leader, and the social chairman, can meet together to conduct class business. Here are some things they will need to discuss:

1 The social calendar needs to be discussed.

2 Evaluation needs to be made as to whether the class units are "outreaching."

3 Discussion of class projects should take place.

4 It is good for the class leaders to use some of this time together for prayer on behalf of one another and their class members.

"Well, that's what meetings are all about," Tom finished.

"You know, Tom," Jim said, "if we were meeting like that, I'd really feel more confident about my teaching position. I'd feel like the people in my class were on a team with me. I think the whole idea is great."

"I'll second that," Paul spoke up. "I wouldn't mind serving in some capacity in Sunday school if I knew I wouldn't be floundering around by myself all the time. And these meetings would see to it that I had some help and guidance."

"Looks like we're all sold on staff meetings," Tom smiled.

"I thought of something during the week that I'd like to ask," Sandy offered.

"What is it, Sandy?" Tom questioned her.

"Well, I was wondering what part the actual room we meet in has to do with all this. I mean, can it improve our Sunday school situation to improve the environment we're meeting in?"

"Sandy, you must be a mind reader!" Tom laughed. "That's going to be our topic for next week. We're going to see how we can increase our effectiveness by improving our classroom environment. You'd be surprised how much a room does influence learning and fellowship."

FOOTNOTE

CHAPTER FIVE

1 · Ephesians 4:12, *New American Standard Bible.* ᶜ The Lockman Foundation, 1971. Used by permission.

WHERE ARE WE GOING
TO DO ALL THIS

The Taylors, Hamiltons, and Sanders were feeling pretty chipper. They knew that in the last few weeks they had covered quite a bit of material pertaining to Sunday school. They had discussed:

1 Objectives
2 Organization
3 Leadership
4 Creation of departments and divisions
5 Planning meetings.

"We're really moving along!" Tom said enthusiastically. "And today we're going to discuss something very vital to any successful Sunday school: the environment in which we place our adults for effective learning."

"You know what excites me, Tom?" Jim asked. "It's putting all these new ideas and plans into action as soon as we can."

"Me too," Paul agreed. "I'm anxious to see the improvement in our Sunday school once we start using our new-found information."

"Patience, brethren, patience," Tom smiled. "There are still a few more things to learn!"

WHY FACILITIES ARE IMPORTANT

It's time to look at the physical setting in which the Sunday school is to operate. The environment in which classes function can be very vital in shaping the effectiveness of Sunday school as a whole. There are several reasons for the importance of the facilities for adults.

STRATEGIC POSITION
OF ADULT DEPARTMENT

The educational facilities for adults are important because the adult department of the Sunday school is strategic to the entire program of the local church. Ironically, provision for adults is often the forgotten element in the church building program. The result: Adults wind up using such places as the pastor's study, the choir loft, the kitchen in the fellowship hall, the sanctuary, the furnace room—almost any place they can be crowded into. This is most unfortunate, for the adult department of the Sunday school can be the key to the numerical growth of the entire school as well as the primary source from which to draw leadership for teaching, superintending, and for filling positions on the various boards and committees in the rest of the church organization.

INVOLVEMENT IN
SUNDAY SCHOOL OBJECTIVES

A second reason that the physical facilities are so important is that three of the four objectives of the adult Sunday school take place primarily in the classroom setting. The production of an atmosphere of warmth and acceptance, the provision of sound biblical instruction, and the provision of a framework for transforming biblical truth into living action all take place within the physical setting of the classroom.

"Well, there's something new I've learned," Linda said. "I always thought you could meet anywhere and get along."

"That's about all you *will* do is get along," Tom informed her. "But you certainly won't get ahead."

SOME GUIDELINES FOR ADULT FACILITIES

There are certain things to be aware of in planning and creating an adult classroom. Let's take a look at some of those guidelines so that it will be easier to create an effective room situation.

FLOOR SPACE

The first thing to be considered is the matter of floor space. Ideally, there should be ten square feet per person in the classroom. With a class size of 30 members, about 300 square feet will be needed in each classroom. The need for maximum involvement in the learning process dictates within broad limits how this 300 square feet should be proportioned. An absurd illustration of this would be a classroom with the dimensions of 5 feet by 60 feet. There would be 300 square feet, all right, but obviously group discussion, circle response, buzz groups, and other such types of group learning experiences would become a comedy of errors and the epitome of chaos and confusion.

On the other hand, dimensions approximating 15 by 20 feet would be much more flexible and usable for learning purposes. Using one of the 20 foot sides as the "front" of the room would work best.

LOCATION OF ROOMS

In addition to the amount of floor space planned per person, another consideration should be the location of the classrooms. Some of the age-level needs of adults should be reflected in the choice of location for their classrooms. Rooms for adults with small children are best located near these children's classrooms. Classrooms for older adults are best placed on the ground floor. (An alternative to this would be the installation of an elevator for their use.) Stairs can be a problem for some older members who have arthritis, cardiac problems, or other health limitations.

LIGHTING AND VENTILATION

It is important that classrooms have the proper lighting, heating, cooling, and ventilation. It has been suggested that there be an illumination level of 30 footcandles in the classroom, that a temperature of 68-70 defrees Fahrenheit be maintained, and that the rate of ventilation be in the neighborhood of 10 cubic feet of air per pupil per minute, while providing 6 to 10 complete changes of air per hour.

ACOUSTICS

Acoustical considerations are also important. The walls of the classroom should be soundproof, the ceiling acoustically treated, and the floor carpeted. Thirty-five to forty decibels has been suggested as the highest acceptable room noise level. Sharp handclaps sounded while the class is in the room should produce no echo. An echo under these conditions means too much reverberation, and additional acoustical treatment would then be necessary. This is particularly important because of the need for moving chairs around for small group learning experiences such as buzz groups, neighbor nudging, etc.

The use of audiovisual aids such as tape recorders, slide, filmstrip or motion picture projectors, and overhead and/or opaque projectors will necessitate having electrical outlets conveniently placed in the room. There also needs to be an efficient and effective means of darkening the room when using projected visuals and for balancing artificial and natural light. (Overhead projectors, however, can be used effectively without altering the normal room light.)

STORAGE

Storage space in our classrooms is necessary in the form of a cabinet or some sort of a closet. Chalk, eraser, paper, pencils, and other materials which might be needed during the class session may be kept there.

Up to this point only the permanent or nonmovable aspects of the physical facilities have been discussed. But what about the equipment that goes into this well-planned classroom space?

CHAIRS AND TABLES

Certainly there should be sufficient chairs for the number

who will be attending the class. They should be movable so that circles, squares, and discussion groups may be formed easily and quickly. Some find it advantageous to buy "tablet chairs" which have a large arm rest suitable for taking notes, stacking books, and so forth.

It will be helpful to the teacher if there is a small table available on which to place his Bible and other teaching materials (not to be used as a podium, however). A second small table or desk can be of help to the secretary as a place to centralize his clerical activities.

CHALKBOARD

Many teachers are handicapped without a chalkboard. Either a permanent or a portable one should be provided in the classroom. A tack board or bulletin board also can be a useful teaching tool for displaying visual aids, emphasizing announcements, or describing service projects. If an overhead projector is frequently used, it is well to have a permanent screen in the classroom.

SEATING ARRANGEMENT

It is important to recognize that the arrangement of the equipment within the facilities will have an important effect on creating an atmosphere of warmth and acceptance. The back of heads and an occasional profile view do little to promote fellowship and personal interaction among class members. But putting the chairs in a large circle helps to create an atmosphere of warmth and acceptance because it allows each student to face another as well as to have his neighbor partially face him. The desired atmosphere of warmth and acceptance can be enhanced even more by breaking the large group up into smaller units for discussion and exchange of ideas. This promotes participation, self-knowledge, and knowledge of the other people in the group as well. Also, it is easier for latecomers to enter these groups if they are already formed before their arrival.

"I see now what you mean about the environment playing such a big part in our learning," Jim commented. "It really makes sense to me."

"Wait, there's more!" Tom said. "But first let's review what we've discussed already."

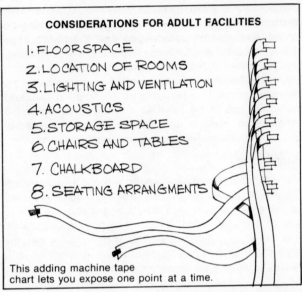

CONSIDERATIONS FOR ADULT FACILITIES

1. FLOORSPACE
2. LOCATION OF ROOMS
3. LIGHTING AND VENTILATION
4. ACOUSTICS
5. STORAGE SPACE
6. CHAIRS AND TABLES
7. CHALKBOARD
8. SEATING ARRANGMENTS

This adding machine tape chart lets you expose one point at a time.

"Now let's discuss more personal matters relating to creating this atmosphere of warmth and acceptance," Tom went on.

SOME PERSONAL FACTORS FOR CREATING WARMTH AND ACCEPTANCE

Many of the things that are done or not done in Sunday school can either help create or destroy a feeling of warmth and acceptance that is sought after. Let's look at several of these factors.

FELLOWSHIP TIME

Although the facilities should be made conducive to creating an atmosphere of warmth and acceptance, the real creators of this desired atmosphere are the students themselves. New people should be made to feel welcome, their names correctly ascertained, and their introduction to the group handled with warmth, confidence, and thoughtfulness. It is helpful to provide a fellowship time before, or preferably after, the class session so that the class members and visitors can become better acquainted, continue their exchange of ideas, and develop and deepen their friendship. If the facilities permit the serving of coffee and doughnuts or similar refreshments, this should be done; it helps to make this time of social interaction more relaxing and enjoyable.

TEACHER'S ROLE

It cannot be emphasized too much how strategic the teacher's role is in producing this atmosphere of warmth and acceptance. For instance, when the class is to be divided up into smaller discussion groups or other changes are to be made in the physical setup, the teacher should offer the directives in a friendly manner which will elicit a cooperative response on the part of everyone involved. Frequent changes in the room setup will produce an air of expectancy and curiosity which will make the class time a highly enjoyable event. The teacher can help shy students feel comfortable and willing to participate by drawing them out with questions while at the same time being careful not to criticize or make fun of any statement that has been made. Keeping the question, "What's happening to people?" ever before him is helpful in keeping him from doing anything which might further inhibit participation of a student in the class time activities.

"We need to remember that adults learn best when the atmosphere is one which encourages them to be instrumental in problem-solving or when they are stimulated by an interest or challenge," Tom said. "They need to be personally involved in experiences in which they must think, talk, and work together in discovering and applying biblical truth. They need to feel that they are making progress together in fulfilling the purpose of the class or lesson."

"I get it!" Jim jumped in. "And in order for this to be accomplished, there must be an atmosphere of warmth and acceptance present."

"Right," Tom agreed. "But this doesn't happen by accident. It must be carefully planned for and continuously created by the careful use of facilities and equipment and by each class member walking 'in love, as Christ also hath loved us. . . .' "[1]

"You know," Vicki recalled, "I can remember when I was younger that I went into a Sunday school classroom where I didn't know anyone. It was a cold, unfeeling atmosphere, and the kids in the class didn't make matters any better. And I hated that class the whole hour I was there. I never went back."

"And I can remember going to a new church as a collegian," Paul added. "I was scared to death of the new people I'd meet, but after five minutes in that classroom, I felt great! I stayed in that church for three years, and some of those classmates in that Sunday school class are still friends of mine."

"You see, then, how significant environment is to our learning and our feelings of acceptance," Tom said. "We all have to work to make the classroom environment what it should be."

"What's next on the learning agenda, Tom?" Jim wanted to know.

"Well, next week I thought we'd go over the duties of the class officers a little more thoroughly. There's some material I've recently discovered that will clear up their duties and really let us know in depth what they do and how they do it. And then the week after next, I have a big surprise for all of you!"

"A surprise! What is it?" Linda wanted to know.

"Yes, tell us, Tom!" Vicki agreed.

"No dice," Tom smiled. "I want to make sure you're all coming back next week—and the week after that—so I think I'll keep you in suspense for those two weeks. See you next Tuesday night right here again!"

FOOTNOTE

CHAPTER SIX

1 · Ephesians 5:2, KJV

HOW CAN WE DO OUR JOBS?

"One of the things which has been a problem for many Sunday schools," Tom began the following week, "is how to help the class officers do their jobs efficiently."

"Most of the time people don't even know *what* they're supposed to do, much less how to do it," Jim commented.

"Which must be pretty frustrating," Paul added.

"But it's just as frustrating to know what you're supposed to do and not know *how* to do it," Tom said. "And that's what we're going to talk about tonight."

"Then comes the surprise, right?" Sandy questioned, smiling.

"Patience, Sandy, patience. That comes next week—at our final meeting," Tom informed her. "First things first, though. Let's look again at our class leaders, see what they're supposed to be doing, and how they can do their jobs most efficiently and effectively."

THE UNIT LEADER

Let's look once more at the functions of the unit leader. His jobs are:

1 Caring for the members of his unit.
2 Making unit relationships meaningful.

3 Encouraging sharing and understanding among his unit members.

Now let's look at some of the ways the unit leader can perform his functions effectively.

1 The unit leader should make sure that the people in his unit become close friends in Christ. He does this by personally knowing as much as possible about the individuals in his unit. He should contact each unit member or couple weekly. He maintains the contact between all the members of his unit and strives to create the kinds of sharing and caring friendships that are conducive to Christian fellowship.

2 The unit leader should see to it that the unit members have an opportunity to meet together as a unit on a casual or informal basis; it may simply be a spontaneous cup of coffee or lunch after church. Or perhaps some unit members can get together for fellowship during the week. The unit leader, during these times of fellowship, encourages the open and honest communication that characterizes deep fellowship in Christ. Unit members should grow to love and understand one another; they should be aware of one another's problems, perplexities, frustrations, joys, victories in Christ, hobbies. In other words, they should know one another as persons so they can pray for one another intelligently. Spontaneous Bible study or discussion of Sunday morning's Bible lesson may take place among the unit members as they meet together outside of class.

3 The unit leader encourages this kind of support in prayer and fellowship by having them share themselves with one another. When a unit member has a difficulty, it should be the natural thing for him to contact either his unit leader or one of the members of his unit. There should be such a closeness and mutual understanding among all of the members that this action would be almost reflexive. The atmosphere of each unit should be such as to impart the feeling that the people who care most about an individual are the other members of his unit. This is the kind of love which Jesus Christ talked about when He said, ''By this all men will know that you are My disciples, if you have love for one another.''[1]

4 The unit leader makes sure that each member of his unit is present in Sunday school. He should also say a word or two to each one on Sunday morning. It is his responsibility to make sure they are aware of any class or department socials. He should make his unit members feel that he is glad to see them anytime or anyplace.

5 The unit leader is responsible for doing some follow-up if a unit member is absent from Sunday school or a social gathering. This should be done with a loving, concerned attitude rather than as a truant officer doing his duty.

6 It should be the natural thing that when unit members bring a friend to Sunday school, one of the first people they will want to introduce that friend to will be their unit leader. The unit leader should be warm and cordial to that guest and make him feel welcome and wanted. He is also responsible for making sure that the secretary has a record of the visitor's name, address, and phone number. The unit leader should also make it a point to invite the guest to a future social event, and back to Sunday school.

7 The unit leader should make it a point to pray regularly for the people in his unit and the visitors to Sunday school.

8 There are many, many ways in which a unit leader can function. He must use his creativity. He must think of ways he can communicate love and concern and the fact that he cares about the members of his unit. In a real sense he is teaching the members of his unit what it is to be a unit leader. For many of them, when they think of a unit leader, and what he does, they will think of him. He then becomes a pattern of what a unit leader is and does.

THE CLASS LEADER

The class leader, as we have seen, has some very important jobs to carry out:

1 He establishes the class units.

2 He welcomes visitors and acts as host.

3 He works closely with the unit leaders to see that all is functioning well within the class.

4 He presides over the class business and makes the necessary announcements.

5 He may lead the class in hymn singing or other worship activities prior to or after the Bible study time.

How can the class leader effectively do his job?

1 Ministering to others is a personal thing. The class leader must know the people in his class if he is to have a meaningful ministry to them. He may already know all the people or it may take a few months before he feels familiar with everyone.

2 Although he ministers to the entire class, the people who need his ministry the most are the unit leaders. If he is not acquainted with all the people in the class, the first ones to really get to know are the unit leaders. They do what the class leader and the teacher are unable to do—minister in depth to the people in the class. So the class leader must help the unit leaders to have a successful ministry.

3 When a visitor is brought to Sunday school by one of the class members, the class leader ministers to that person along with the unit leader. Also, if a visitor comes by himself—not at the invitation of a class member—it is the class leader who makes him feel welcome, sees that he is registered properly with the class secretary, and is introduced to the rest of the class.

4 It is impractical to try to assign a visitor to a unit on the first Sunday he attends. There isn't enough time to handle that without neglecting other Sunday morning responsibilities. Assignment to a unit can be made during the week. The class leader should contact the unit's leader so he will know that the new person is in his unit. The following Sunday the class leader should introduce the visitor to his unit leader so that contact is made between them. Of course, the class leader informs the secretary of all the assignments so that the records can be kept straight.

5 In this sense, the class leader coordinates with the class secretary in establishing the class units. It is perfectly acceptable to have close friends as members of the same unit. After all, units are attempting to promote

fellowship and unity, not destroy it! However, it is up to the class leader to appraise the composition of each unit—in cooperation with the unit leaders—to make sure that there is a rather even distribution of leadership among, and freedom from cliques within, the various units. To have one unit well stocked with leadership while leaving another to flounder leaderless is disastrous. If unit members are such "good friends" that their unit is not growing through the introduction of new people into it, it is time for the class leader and the unit leader to evaluate the situation to see if it would be better to transfer people into different units at the end of a quarter.

Obviously this could turn into a problem. As a general principle it is well to change unit membership at the end of each quarter. Everyone changing units each quarter prevents an unproductive unit from becoming an "institution."

6 If possible, the class leader should place visitors in the same unit with the people who brought them. At the end of a quarter or two they may be ready to be part of a unit separate from the friends who originally brought them.

7 The class leader should keep in weekly contact with the unit leaders so that he knows exactly what is happening within each unit.

8 The class leader takes the initiative in establishing the atmosphere of warmth and acceptance which should characterize the Sunday morning class time. As people arrive before class time, he should mix and mingle with them. This time should be a relaxing and enjoyable prelude to the study of God's Word. He should introduce himself to visitors. If the visitors were brought by a class member, the class leader should be sure to introduce them to the member's unit leader. He should also introduce them to the class secretary so that needed information may be obtained.

9 The class leader should see to it that all of the relevant announcements are made. In most cases this should be done before the Bible study time. These announcements should be kept to a minimum, since time on Sunday morning is precious.

10 The class leader should occasionally provide time for a unit leader to share a successful unit activity with the rest of the class. It will stimulate other units into action and give them some good ideas on what to do. It need be nothing more than a brief testimony over the coffee cup, discussion of the previous week's Bible study, or a meaningful time shared in visitation.

11 Many churches enjoy singing a hymn or two prior to the teaching/learning time. The class leader either leads this singing himself or recruits another to do it for him. In either case, the hymns that are sung should relate to the morning's Bible lesson as much as possible. Consider the singing to be a part of the total teaching of the morning, not something to be done to pass the time before the teacher takes over the class. Avoid "Does anyone have a favorite for us to sing?" Most people don't have a favorite on the tip of their tongue, and time is wasted looking through the hymnbook. Hymns should be deliberately chosen to prepare the class for an encounter with the Lord through the study of His Word.

12 If an offering is taken in Sunday school, the class leader should make sure that this is done reverently, as an act of worship. He should ask class members for prayer requests. These requests should be mentioned to God as the prayer is spoken before receiving the Sunday school offering. People are thereby given the assurance that the class is praying for them corporately and that the class cares for one another. And the offering becomes one of mutual sharing and worship as well.

THE CLASS SECRETARY

The duties of the class secretary are:
1 Maintaining the class roll, which also functions as a mailing list.
2 Assisting the class leader in placing new members into a unit.
3 Counting the offering and taking it to the proper place.
4 Cultivating the visitors by sending them a short letter stating that the class was pleased to have them in at-

tendance and invites them to return the next week.

5 Cooperating with the social chairman in promoting the class social functions.

6 Sending an absentee card during the week following a person's absence.

It is practically impossible for a class to function without a secretary who does his job well. The other class leaders are highly dependent on the class secretary because of the importance of the data which the secretary keeps at his fingertips.

1 The careful records maintained by the class secretary help the class leader and the unit leaders to assess the progress made by the class units. It would be impossible to construct plans for future growth without the data which the class secretary provides.

2 The class secretary does not need to know all of the class members to take the attendance rolls on Sunday morning. But he should be acquainted with the unit leaders so that they can assist in the roll taking by telling the secretary who is absent from their unit. Before long the secretary should know everyone in the class and won't be as dependent on the unit leaders.

3 The class secretary should be warm and friendly as visitors are introduced to him. He should show genuine interest in them as people as he writes down their names, addresses, and phone numbers. This process should not become a mere mechanical one of data recordings, since real people are being dealt with, not computer cards.

4 Having the class secretary in charge of counting and delivering the offering frees the class leader from a detail which could distract him from his work in keeping the class moving along.

5 It might be wise to have the class leader's signature on letters to visitors thanking them for coming and urging them to come again.

6 The supervision of mailed promotional pieces is the class secretary's job, but it does not mean that he should be stuck with doing all of the addressing. The class unit leaders can be called upon to address the pieces going to their unit members.

7 Although the absentees will be contacted by their

unit leaders, it is a nice gesture to have the class secretary send an absentee card during the week also. This card is another way of saying, "We missed you and we really want you to come back as soon as you can." It is another way of saying "We care" and of providing the atmosphere of warmth and acceptance which is to characterize the Sunday school.

THE SOCIAL CHAIRMAN

The social chairman's main function is to supervise the social activities and events of his class. At first glance, this task appears formidable. "Wow! I've gotta throw a party once a month for the entire class? I'll never make it!" may be the reaction of someone who has been asked to take on this responsibility.

But it's not as difficult as it first appears. It doesn't have to be done alone.

1 Since the social chairman's ministry is primarily a supervisory one, he shouldn't do all of the work. But he does have to make sure that all of the work is done by someone! He should feel free to work with the class unit leaders and assign a unit to be responsible for a social. Next month a different unit can do it. Or perhaps two units could work in cooperation with each other in planning an event. The point is that the social chairman should not be afraid to activate other class members. This is one of the major roles of the social chairman.

2 He should avoid having the same people do the work month after month. He is to oversee and coordinate the efforts of the other class members in putting on the monthly socials.

"Well," said Tom, "that does it. Of course, it is impossible to list all of the things which the class leaders can do to fulfill their responsibilities. I was just trying to whet your appetites for being a class leader and to stimulate your creative thinking concerning some of the ways in which you as a leader could help our Sunday school achieve its objectives."

"Well, you sure succeeded in doing that," Paul commented. "I'm ready to get to work right now."

Everyone nodded his head. "We all want to get to work, Tom," Jim spoke up. "We've heard from you how to organize a Sunday school, how to use leadership effectively, how to make the room environment work for you instead of against you, and how to plan for your sessions. I think we'd all agree that we really want to help. We want to see something exciting happen in our Sunday school. We want to see God use us in a mighty way."

"I couldn't be happier, Jim," Tom responded. "I know how much time you've all put into these meetings. And I realize how excited you are about Sunday school now. And believe me, I'm excited about *your* excitement. That's where it all begins, you know, in a person's willingness to be used by God in His work. I know you all have that willingness."

"Hey, you mentioned that surprise for next week," Vicki said. "Is it still on?"

"You bet," Tom answered her. "I think I've got something planned for you for next week that will top off our Sunday school study perfectly."

"Sounds fascinating," Jim said. "I won't even ask if we can all be here—since the look on everyone's face has already answered that question."

As the couples said good night and went on their ways home, each person was anticipating the surprise that Tom had prepared for them for next week.

But more than that, each was anticipating the forthcoming changes in their Sunday school—changes which would make that organization a more effective tool for the Lord.

FOOTNOTE

CHAPTER SEVEN

1 · John 13:35, *New American Standard Bible*. © The Lockman Foundation, 1971. Used by permission.

CHAPTER EIGHT

GETTING IT ALL TOGETHER

The following week, Tom Sanders showed up to present his surprise—five of them! He came in with five people following him. As they all sat down in the Taylors' living room, Tom introduced his guests.

"These are some friends of mine from various churches in our community," he said. "John and Virginia Adrian have been attending a Sunday school that has independent class meetings. I thought you would like to hear what goes on in their particular Sunday school sessions. Roy and Marcie Rawlins attend a Sunday school class which also meets with the adult department for an assembly time. They have some interesting things to say. And Mark Riley teaches a class in an elective Sunday school system. He's going to tell us how that works. In this way, I thought we might see a little more clearly how these three setups for Sunday school classes operate. What do you say?"

"Brilliant!" Jim exclaimed. "I'm excited about hearing how other Sunday schools work."

The approval of Tom's "surprise" was unanimous. As Virginia and John Adrian talked about their Sunday school time, the Taylors and Hamiltons listened enthusiastically, eager to learn all they could about procedures.

THE INDEPENDENT CLASS MEETING

As Virginia and John Adrian ascend the steps to their Sunday school class, the church Sunday school bus slows to a halt in the parking lot, making a familiar "chirp, chirp, chirp" sound.

"I guess squeaky brakes are better than no brakes at all," John quips to his wife.

"Yes," she replies. "Look how excited those kids are as they go off to their Sunday school departments. Isn't it great to see kids excited about Sunday school?"

Virginia and John enter their Sunday school classroom, and are greeted by the aroma of brewing coffee. Several other couples are already there, chatting comfortably with one another as they hold white styrofoam coffee cups in their hands. Virginia and John join two of the other couples in the class unit.

"Long time no see," says John.

"Hours!" agrees Lance Goodson. "Sure do appreciate that fine dinner we had at your home last night. I might add that the fellowship was delightful too."

"We certainly enjoyed having you folks over," responds Virginia. "It's good to get to know you better. There's no telling how long we would have remained strangers if they hadn't organized our classes into units," Virginia continues with a chuckle.

"Jim and Bonnie were just telling us," Lance offers, "of Jim's new promotion at work."

"Well, congratulations! I'm happy for you. We have a note of praise this morning! Have you told our unit leader? I'm sure he'll want to tell Pete so the whole class can share in your joy."

"No, don't go spreading that around," Jim resists. "It will sound like I'm bragging or something."

"Bragging, nothing!" John retorts. "We know that you know that the Lord gave you that promotion. You'll let us share in thanking Him so that the whole class can rejoice with you, won't you?"

"Well, since you put it that way . . ." Jim replies.

Pete Miller, the class leader, interrupts by asking the class to find a seat and turn to hymn number 18, "Thank

We Now All the Father, Who In His Grace Gives Out Promotions to Those Who Need It the Most" (based on an obscure psalm).

As the class starts to sing, two new figures appear in the doorway. Arnold Turner, a unit leader, quietly walks over to them and shakes hands with the visitors.

"Hi! Arnie's my name," he says in a low voice. "Glad you can be with us today. We're the Berean Class."

Pete Miller had asked Arnie ahead of time to greet late-coming visitors in his stead so that it would not interrupt the entire class.

"I'd like you folks to meet Mary Evans, our class secretary," Arnie continues in a semiwhisper.

"Hello," says Mary warmly. "I'm happy you can be with us today. Did you just recently move into town?"

"No, we're just passing through on vacation," the visitors reply.

"Would you be so kind as to fill out our visitor registration form?" Mary asks.

The visitors comply.

Arnie chats briefly with them and shows them to a seat toward the back of the classroom.

Pete Miller concludes the song service and mentions that there are some visitors today. "Arnie, will you introduce these folks to us, please?"

"Glad to, Pete," Arnie responds enthusiastically. "This is Fred and Nancy Perkins. Fred has been with the Wabash Corporation, an electronics firm, for four years as a maintenance man. He and Nancy are passing through on their way to Lake Montgomery to do some fishing on their vacation. Sam, you'd probably like to get together with Fred after class and debate the merits of dry-fly versus wet-fly fishing."

The class chuckles and some look knowingly over at Sam.

"Sam's caught some big ones at the lake," Pete affirms. "We hope that you'll be able to stop back on your way home and visit us again. We're happy that you're here today and we wish you a warm and cordial welcome in the name of Christ.

"Art Harrigan tells me that we have reason to rejoice with one of his unit members, Jim Smith, who received a promotion at work. We rejoice with you, Jim, and will pray with you that this will open up new areas of witness for our Lord.

"Before we receive the morning offering, I'd like to share with you some needs for you to include on your private prayer list. Sally Smithers found out this week that her four-year-old daughter, Melanie, is going to need open-heart surgery.

"Are there any other requests? Perhaps you didn't have a chance to talk to your unit leader, and consequently I am not informed of the need," Pete encourages.

"I have a note of praise," volunteers a class member. "You recall that fellow at the office that I started cultivating several months ago—Duane Stevens is his name. During our noon hour Bible study at work he received the Saviour. He's born again, and since so many of you have been praying for his salvation, I thought maybe we as a class could thank God together for answered prayer."

"That's tremendous!" Pete responds. "Let's bow together for a word of prayer.

"Father, we thank you that you are the giver of every good and perfect gift. We rejoice with Jim and Bonnie Smith because of the promotion you have provided for him. And we pray, God, that this promotion will be used for your honor and glory.

"And then, Lord, we thank you for the gift of eternal life that you have given us through Christ. We thank you for answered prayer in granting this gift to Duane Stevens.

"You know the need that little Melanie Smithers has. Grant her your perfect peace, and may your comfort be the portion of her parents as well. Guide the hand of the surgeon; raise up this little one to perfect health and a lifelong ministry of serving Christ.

"Father, you've given us so much; and now we give because you first gave to us. Accept this offering, we pray, as a token of our love and worship. We pray that others will come to Christ as a result of this financial stewardship. Prepare our hearts for the study of your Word, and we'll thank you for it. In Jesus' name. Amen.

USE OF CLASS SESSION TIME

	Preparation for Study	Bible Study	Response
INDEPENDENT CLASS	**15-20 minutes** for fellowship, sharing joys and burdens, introducing visitors, prayer, offering and singing	**30-45 minutes** for Bible study featuring methods which actively involve the students	**5-10 minutes** for individuals to greet and welcome visitors, more fellowship and informal discussion of the lesson

	Preparation for Study	Bible Study	Response
DEPARTMENT MEETING	**10-15 minutes** for coffee and fellowship, department superintendent leads in singing a hymn and makes necessary announcements, visitors introduced, offering taken	**30-45 minutes** for introducing visitors to individual class, visitor information secured by class secretary, and Bible study featuring methods which actively involve the students	**5-10 minutes** for the same as above

		Bible Study	Response
ELECTIVES		**30-45 minutes** for Bible study featuring methods which actively involve the students, class chosen by the individual, visitors introduced and identified by age group	**15-30 minutes** to return to "home-base" class, visitors escorted by class member, visitors introduced, announcements made, prayer requests, offering, singing and fellowship time

"Before Len Cole leads us in our Bible study, I'd like to remind you of the class social next Friday night. The progressive dinner starts at the Clayborn's at 6:30. See Mary if you haven't made your reservations.

"Len, lead us in the study of the Word, would you please?"

Len spreads out his teaching materials on the small table at the front of the classroom and begins his instructions to the class members.

"Today we're going to discuss dealing with your enemies. Let's start out with some 'neighbor nudging.' Discuss with the person next to you for one minute the answer to this question: 'How do you think David felt when he cut off the skirt of Saul's robe?' "

After the minute is up, Len lists some of the answers the class members give to the question.

Len then leads the class into several different types of learning experiences: a third of the class researches the background of the David/Saul incident; another third looks at the teachings of Jesus on how to deal with enemies; the remainder of the class studies Philemon to see what principles of love and brotherhood are taught in that book. Len leads the discussion, listing the groups' findings on the chalkboard. The class then observes a roleplay of how to deal with "enemies."

Len closes the class session with prayer.

Pete Miller, the class leader, seeks out the Perkinses and says to them, "Sure glad you could be with us today. Please come back if you can.

"Are you planning on attending our morning worship service?"

"Yes, we are," Fred Perkins answers.

"How about coming with me to the primary department? I'd like you to meet my wife, Joan. She teaches a Sunday school class there. She'd like to meet you folks. If you'd like, we can all sit together in church."

"We'd like that," Fred responded. "You lead the way."

"Wow!" Jim responded to the Adrian's story of their Sunday school session. "You certainly get a lot accomplished!"

"And everyone is so friendly," Sandy responded. "The Perkinses must have loved meeting all the class members. They were really put at ease with the way things ran."

"I thought you might enjoy hearing about an independent class," Tom said. "Now let's review in our minds the order of events in this class situation."

IN SUMMARY

Here, then, are the events which took place in the independent class meetings:

1 A fellowship time with coffee for each individual class. This includes sharing of interesting and exciting events which took place during the week and prayer requests.

2 The class session begins with the singing of a hymn.

3 Late-coming visitors are greeted by a unit leader so that the class leader does not have to interrupt the song which he is leading.

4 The class secretary has visitors fill out a registration form so that an accurate record can be kept of their names and addresses.

5 Visitors are introduced to the entire class and are personally welcomed by the class leader.

6 The class leader presents to the class those people and happenings to be prayed for during the week and shares blessings that have occurred with the rest of the class.

7 Class members are urged to request prayer or share a particular blessing in their lives.

8 The class leader leads the class in a time of prayer.

9 A class offering is taken while announcements of upcoming events are made.

10 The teacher brings the lesson to the rest of the class, being sure to include active participation on the part of every member.

11 The teacher closes the lesson with prayer.

12 As the class breaks up, the class members make a special point of seeking out visitors and welcoming them, while encouraging them to return if at all possible.

Perhaps someone in the class might suggest sitting with the visitors during the service so that they might know someone in the congregation.

"Now," Tom continued, "Marcie and Roy Rawlins are going to relate to us what happens in their class on Sunday mornings. In their situation, the classes meet together for a department meeting and then go to smaller groups. Roy, I'll let you tell the group what happens in your Sunday school."

THE ADULT CLASSES COMBINE FOR A DEPARTMENT MEETING

Marcie and Roy Rawlins are enjoying the coffee fellowship prior to being dismissed for the Young Marrieds Bible study time.

"I really like this time of fellowship before going to our class," Marcie comments to her husband. "I enjoy feeling a part of all of the adults."

"It's great to get to know people's names so that we can associate them with their faces," Roy agrees. "We could attend church for years and never meet half the people we do if it weren't for this time Sunday morning.

"I'm amazed at the spunk of some of those folks we call senior citizens. They gave you younger fellows a run for your money yesterday when we painted Mrs. Johnson's house."

"Don't rub it in; I bet they have as many sore muscles as we do!" Roy chides.

Steve Tyson, the department superintendent, nods to the pianist, and he plays a familiar hymn. Conversation ebbs as people find seats.

The singing ends and Steve makes some announcements. "It looks like the Friendship Class shot us younger folk out of the saddle again this month. They had a higher percentage of their class out to participate in yesterday's service project.

"For those of you who couldn't make it, we succeeded in getting widow Johnson's house completely painted on the outside. And you wouldn't believe the lunch the women had for us. We asked the blessing, but I think we should have asked for forgiveness! We all had a great time and we were able to express the love of Christ in a concrete way at the same time. Next week we'll be telling you about our adult service project for next month.

"I'd like to call upon our class leaders to introduce any visitors we may have with us today," the department superintendent said.

"Steve, I'd like to introduce Judy and Paul Lane. They recently moved into the Offenhausers' neighborhood and are visiting our Young Marrieds class. I met them last Thursday night when my unit was doing some visitation. The Lanes have two children. Paul likes to play golf when he isn't doing the accounting for the Selwood Lumber Company."

"A hearty welcome to the Lanes," Steve says.

Steve continues, "I would like to share several prayer requests with you. You can pray for these individually and as classes. Let's continue to pray for our church's evangelistic services. Martha Webber fell this week and broke her hip. Each of the class secretaries has the address of the hospital she is in; so let's all send her a get-well card and remember her in prayer."

Steve leads the department in prayer and the offering is received. After the offertory is finished, Steve announces that the classes are dismissed to their Bible study time.

Mark Stevens, the Young Marrieds class leader, is introduced to the Lanes by the Offenhausers' unit leader. Mark in turn introduces the Lanes to George Kant, the Young Marrieds class secretary. The Offenhausers' unit leader seats the Lanes next to the Offenhausers.

Class time is characterized by several kinds of learning experiences. The teacher calls upon one of the unit leaders to close the Bible study time in prayer.

It scarcely seems possible that Sunday school can be over so quickly!

"That's another good setup," Paul commented when the Rawlinses had finished discussing their particular Sunday school.

"Still one more to go," Tom added, "but first let's review the Rawlinses schedule in Sunday school."

IN SUMMARY

Here is a summary of what took place in a Sunday school situation in which the adult classes combine for a department meeting:

1 A short coffee fellowship time before the Bible study time prepares people to study God's Word together in a warm, comfortable environment.

2 A hymn is sung to signal that the coffee fellowship time is over. Those standing around or sitting should find seats. The hymn is usually led by the department superintendent.

3 The department superintendent makes announcements to the entire adult department. Visitors are also introduced at this point. These may be introduced by the various class leaders who have met the visitors during the coffee fellowship.

4 The department superintendent shares prayer requests and then leads the department in a short, meaningful prayer.

5 An offering is taken.

6 The adults are then dismissed to go to their Bible study time consisting of smaller class groups.

7 In the classes, the class leader should introduce the visitors to the class teacher. The class secretary would then obtain the necessary information for the visitors.

8 The actual Bible study time takes place next. At the close of this time, the teacher either leads or asks someone else to close in prayer.

9 Class members are then dismissed to go to the church service.

"Wow! That sounds like an interesting class," Jim exclaimed.

"I guess we'll have to spend some time deciding which schedule is best for our Sunday school," Sandy said. "They both sound good!"

"Hold on until you've heard the third alternative," Tom said. "Mark Riley is here to tell us about an elective class system which I think you'll all find very interesting. Mark, the floor is yours! We're ready to hear of your Sunday school class."

THE CLASS IN AN ELECTIVE SYSTEM

Mark Riley closed the Bible study period in prayer. "Our Bible study time is over. We now return to our home base classes for a time of fellowship. We do this so that the visitors will get a chance to meet several people in their own age group and get to know them better. We hope you visitors will take the opportunity offered in the home base class—the class which is your particular age group—to get to know some of us better. The class leader and secretary will get the vital information on you—such as your name and address and phone number—in the home base fellowship time.

"Are there any visitors with us today? I'm going to ask a representative from each of our age groups to stand. On your right is Al Stacy. He is from the Young Marrieds class. If you are 25 to 39, follow him to room 'B' for your time of fellowship. Over here is Marv Rinker of the Middle Adult class. If you're 40 to 59, follow him to room 'C.' And if you're 60 or above, you can remain here. John Ogner on your far left is the Older Adults class leader.

"You are dismissed. Hope to see you all next week. Be sure to read all of Ephesians 5 this week."

An enthusiastic murmur fills the air as people scurry to their home base classes. Marv Rinker has met the Himlers, middle adults who are visiting for the first time.

He introduces the Himlers to the class secretary.

"While you're filling out this registration form, may I get you folks a cup of coffee?" Marv offers.

"Yes, thank you," the Himlers reply. "We both take it black."

"After you get your coffee, please be seated," directs Marv. "We don't have much time before the morning service and we need to take care of some business so we can get back to chatting with one another.

"The first thing I'd like to do is introduce Otto and Charlotte Himler. They're here for the first time and were in Mark Riley's course on the Christian home. Otto is a salesman for I. J. Hinman, Incorporated. He knows Frank Murphy, who is in our Young Marrieds class. Make sure you shake hands with Otto and Charlotte before the morning is over. Glad you folks could be here today.

"Stella, you walked in about eighteen inches off the floor this morning. Is there anything you'd like to share with us?"

"Oh, I am just so thrilled about the course being offered on prophecy. This morning we talked about the second coming of our Lord, and it seems to be so very near—we'll be able to see him face-to-face. I guess I just got all 'blessed to pieces!' " Stella replies.

"Christ is coming soon," Marv responds. "And that's another reason for cultivating those prospects. Don't forget our class picnic Saturday at Oak Park. Invite those prospects we all have been praying for. We need to get to know one another."

Marv shares some special prayer requests he has received from the unit leaders and several of the members share additional ones. Marv calls upon one of the unit leaders to lead the class in prayer, and then the offering is taken.

"We have time for one hymn before we get back to the ol' coffee cup. Our Lord is coming soon; let's join in singing a song of consecration, 'Take My Life and Let It Be,' " Marv directs.

The class sings, then rises and begins to form into clusters as unit leaders pass out mimeographed announcements concerning the next class project. Several people invite the Himlers to Saturday's picnic. Class units leave together to attend the worship service.

"Let's summarize what went on in the elective study system," Tom directed.

IN SUMMARY

1 Individuals may select the Bible study class of their choosing according to the subject or book being taught. Each class is taught by a different teacher.

2 At the close of the Bible study time, individuals are sent to their "home base class" for a time of fellowship. A representative from each home base class stands, and visitors are told to follow their particular representative to the class which is their age group.

3 The representative (who is usually the class leader) introduces these visitors to the class secretary when they enter the classroom.

4 The class leader then introduces the visitors and the rest of the class and makes announcements to the class.

5 Prayer requests are shared by members and unit leaders.

6 The offering is taken.

7 If there is time, a hymn is sung to close the home base class time. When the class is officially ended, the class members may go over to visitors and encourage their future attendance.

"We also have an alternate plan," Mark Riley told the listening group. "With the elective system, the class could meet together before Bible study instead of after. But the important thing to remember is this: THERE NEEDS TO BE A HOME BASE CLASS WITH WHICH PEOPLE CAN IDENTIFY AND THROUGH WHICH PEOPLE CAN BE CARED FOR."

"That does it," Tom said as Mark Riley finished talking. "We've seen three different schedules which can be adapted to our Sunday school session. I'm sure you all have opinions on which one our church should adapt, but let's save that particular discussion for a later date. Right now, I'd like to thank these people for coming over and sharing with us."

"I must say just one thing, Tom, before we quit," Jim spoke up. "I think I speak for everyone here when I say that these past few weeks have opened up a world of new things for us. I never thought Sunday school could be made to be so interesting and effective at the same time. I thank you for taking the time to explore Sunday school with us. And I know we're really ready to buckle down and work. We all want our Sunday school to achieve its four objectives. We want to help. We want to see people ministered to and taught in our classes. Thank you for turning our eyes so that we can see this vision."

The Taylors, Hamiltons, and Sanders talked and fellowshipped for a while. Then everyone went home. But each person knew that this was just the beginning of something new and exciting. They had not known that bigger and better things were possible in their Sunday school, and they were thrilled at the prospect of being a part of positive change.

NOW WHAT?

This book has been a guide into organizational and planning methods to insure a more successful, more spiritually productive Sunday school. It has discussed room and equipment, class officers and leaders, schedules for meeting, and Bible study. Putting these principles into practice will enable the Sunday school to reach its four objectives. It will take careful and prayerful planning to make your adult Sunday school more effective in the realm of the Spirit. Take it one step at a time.

1 Communicate your objectives to your adults.

2 Educate your leaders concerning the nature of their ministries.

3 Evaluate your facilities and plan for their improved use.

4 Implement modifications in a gentle, loving way.

5 Rely on the Holy Spirit.

Sharing in the task of producing disciples of Christ and new believers is one of the most rewarding experiences you will ever have. As you see souls mature and grow into the likeness of Jesus Christ, knowing the Sunday school ministry in your church has fostered that growth, you will enjoy one of the greatest thrills of serving Christ here on earth. It should and will be a real celebration of joy!

BIBLIOGRAPHY

Brown, James W., et al. *AV Instruction: Media and Methods.* New York: McGraw-Hill Book Company, 1969.

Coleman, Lyman. *Groups in Action.* Newton, Pennsylvania: The Halfway House, 1968.

Edge, Findley. *Helping the Teacher.* Nashville: Broadman Press, 1959.

Edge, Findley. *Teaching for Results.* Nashville: Broadman Press, 1956.

Ford, LeRoy. *Primer for Teachers and Leaders.* Nashville: Broadman Press, 1963.

Ford, LeRoy. *Tools for Teaching and Training.* Nashville: Broadman Press, 1961.

Ford, LeRoy. *Using the Case Study in Teaching and Training.* Nashville: Broadman Press, 1970.

Ford, LeRoy. *Using the Lecture in Teaching and Training.* Nashville: Broadman Press, 1968.

Ford, LeRoy. *Using the Panel in Teaching and Training.* Nashville: Broadman Press, 1971.

Howard, Walden, ed. *Groups That Work.* Grand Rapids: Zondervan Publishing House, 1967.

Larson, Bruce. *Dare to Live Now.* Grand Rapids: Zondervan Publishing House, 1967.

Larson, Bruce. *The Emerging Church. Grand Rapids: Zondervan Publishing House, 1970.*

Larson, Bruce. *Living on the Growing Edge.* Grand Rapids: Zondervan Publishing House, 1971.

Larson, Bruce. *Marriage Is for Living.* Grand Rapids: Zondervan Publishing House, 1968.

Larson, Bruce. *No Longer Strangers.* Grand Rapids: Zondervan Publishing House, 1971.

Larson, Bruce. *Setting Men Free.* Grand Rapids: Zondervan Publishing House, 1967.

Leypoldt, Martha. *Forty Ways to Teach in Groups.* Valley Forge: Judson Press, 1967.

Leypoldt, Martha. *Learning Is Change.* Valley Forge: Judson Press 1971.

Miller, Keith. *Habitation of Dragons.* Waco: Word Books, 1970.

Miller, Keith and **Auchard,** Lloyd D. *The Second Touch.* Waco: Word Books, 1967.

Miller, Keith. *The Taste of New Wine.* Waco: Word Books, 1965.

Morrison, Eleanor Shelton and Foster, Virgil E. *Creative Teaching in the Church.* Englewood Cliffs: Prentice-Hall Incorporated, 1963.

Pierce, Rice A. *Leading Dynamic Bible Study.* Nashville: Broadman Press, 1969.

Richards, Lawrence. *Creative Bible Teaching.* Chicago: Moody Press, 1970.

Wald, Oletta. *Joy of Discovery.* Minneapolis: Bible Banner Press, 1956.

Wright, H. Norman. *Ways to Help Them Learn Adults.* Glendale: Regal Books, 1971.

SOCIAL/SING PLANNING GUIDE

Here are some suggested purposes for a social/sing. Check the one(s) you feel apply to the events you are planning.

☐ Fun and Fellowship

☐ Introducing new people to the group

☐ Honoring individuals (i.e., going-away parties, installation banquets, etc.)

☐ Evangelism (using the event as an opportunity to set the stage for talking to unbelievers about Christ)

☐ Spiritual growth

☐ Other_____

_____

☐ The primary activity of this event is_____

_____

☐ At this point, how about deciding on a theme for the event_____

_____

Now that you have determined the "why" the next step is to determine the "what" and the "how." What can be done to reach the objectives decided upon? The "how" question is really a "who" question—to whom will the responsibility for the various parts of the program be delegated? Take a quick look at the check list—perhaps it will jar the wheels of your creative thinking into motion.

☐ Time and date of the social/sing_____

_____

☐ Place_____

_____

☐ _____
is in charge of reservations and/or ticket sales.

☐ Transportation arrangements need to be made.
☐ Yes ☐ No ☐ _____
    has been contacted to drive the bus.

The following people will drive their cars:

☐ _____

☐ _____

Will there be a need for decorations?
    ☐ Yes ☐ No   The following people are in charge
      of decorations:

☐ _____

☐ _____

Are there any games being planned?
    ☐ Yes ☐ No

	Game	Supplier and/or Leader
☐	_____	_____
☐	_____	_____

How can this event best be promoted and advertised?

	Media	Person responsible
☐	Lay-out designer for the promotional material	_____
☐	Posters	_____
☐	Pulpit announcement	_____
☐	Newspaper article	_____
☐	Handbills	_____
☐	Telephone campaign	_____
☐	Church bulletin	_____
☐	Other	_____
☐	Appointment made with the church office for ''running off'' the material	_____

        day   date   time

Number of people planned for _____

What costs are associated with this event? Total ÷ by
planned for = cost per-person (non-paying guests
not included in # planned for).

☐ Food _____
☐ Promotion _____
☐ Decorations _____
☐ Program (film?) _____
☐ Honorarium _____
☐ Other _____
      Total $ _____

Will food or refreshments be needed?
   ☐ Yes ☐ No
      Menu   Supplier

  ☐ _____   _____
  ☐ _____   _____

The following people will serve the food:

  ☐ _____ ☐ _____
  ☐ _____ ☐ _____

The program schedule is as follows:

  ☐ From _____ to _____ we will _____
  ☐ From _____ to _____ we will _____

Are there any announcements which should be
made? ☐ Yes ☐ No
    Announcement   Person to make it

_____   _____

_____   _____

☐ _____ will introduce
any visitors at the point in the program indicated above.

☐ _____ has been contact-
ed to lead in prayer (invocation/returning thanks).

Is a devotional speaker in order? ☐ Yes ☐ No.

☐ _____ has been
contacted at least two weeks in advance and will bring
a brief devotional message.

Will a clean-up committee be necessary?
   ☐ Yes ☐ No

The following people are on this committee:

☐ _____

☐ _____

☐ The secretary has been contacted to write thank-you
notes to the following people:

                                    name/addresses

☐ Host and/or hostess   _____

                            _____

☐ Devotional speaker   _____

                            _____

☐ Program "specials"   _____

                            _____

☐ Other   _____

                            _____

☐ Other areas of planning not included in this work
sheet:

MONTHLY/WEEKLY PLANNING GUIDE

Type of meeting:

☐ Sunday school council ☐ Adult department meeting
☐ Adult division meeting ☐ Class leader meeting

Why are we meeting: _____

When are we meeting: _____

Who should attend the

meeting: When were they contacted:

☐ _____   _____
☐ _____   _____
☐ _____   _____
☐ _____   _____

Items for discussion	Discussion leader	When were they notified	Time Allowed

TEACHER'S PLANNING SHEET

Session # _____ Date _____

Scripture Passage _____

My aims for this session are to help me and my students
to:

KNOW _____

FEEL _____

DO _____

Fellowship

Who is in charge? _____

Before or after the session? _____

Class leaders responsible for this session _____

_____

_____

Approach to the Word

Bible Learning Activity Chosen _____

_____

Time Required _____

_____

Materials Required _____

_____

Exposition and Response to the Word

   Bible Learning Activity Chosen _____

_____

   Time Required _____

_____

   Materials Required _____

_____

Conclusion and Decision

   Bible Learning Activity Chosen _____

_____

   Time Required _____

_____

   Materials Required _____

_____

Train for Effective Leadership

The impact of effective leadership can be felt in every area of your Sunday school. Train your leaders and teachers with **Success Handbooks** from ICL. Prepared by recognized authorities in Christian education, the handbooks in each series are especially designed for four basic age groups: **Early Childhood, Children, Youth, Adult.**

Series 1, Ways to Help Them Learn
The Success Handbook on each level discusses the learning process, age characteristics, needs and abilities, plus proven teaching techniques.

Series 2, Ways to Plan and Organize Your Sunday School
The Success Handbook on each level offers guidance in building your Sunday school with a plan consistent and effective at every level.

Each Success Handbook $1.95.
set of all 8: $14.95.

Regal Books
Glendale, California

"**A** teacher has not taught until his pupil has learned."

HENRIETTA MEARS

EVERY TEACHER NEEDS TEACH
the award-winning Christian education magazine

Gospel Light's Sunday School IDEA magazine is packed with workable, teachable ideas.
• Methods, preparation hints and learning activities
• Tips for teaching every age level • Complete workers' conference plans • Practical help for leaders

Published quarterly
Single Copies: 1 to 4 – 75¢ each. 5 or more – 60¢ each.
Group Subscriptions: 5 or more to one address – $2.25 each per year.
Single Subscriptions: 1 year – $3.00; 2 years – $5.25; 3 years – $7.50
Order from your regular Sunday School Supplier.

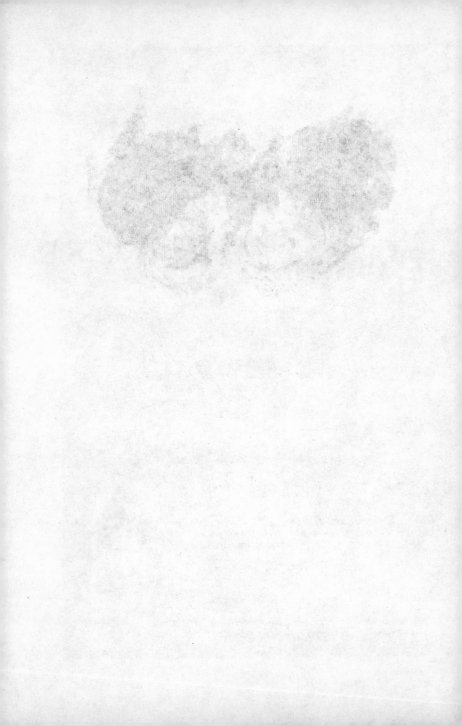